"Edwin Cole brought a worldwide revolution. He emptied himself into us through his books and is ever alive because of the books he's given us."
—**Sunday Adelaja,** Embassy of God, Kiev, Ukraine

"Dr. Cole's ministry helped instill the courage I needed. I encourage you to become the champion God created you to be."
—**A. C. Green**, NBA Ironman

"Ed Cole's books articulate Christlike attributes of manhood that enable men to stand for right and fight against wrong."
—**Tommy Barnett**, Pastor, Phoenix First Assembly

"Ed Cole was a man's man. He could speak to men about their responsibilities, and we listened. What a gift from Heaven when God gave us Ed Cole."
—**Loren Cunningham,** Founder,
Youth With A Mission, Kona

"God brings men onto the scene to make a difference. Dr. Ed Cole was one of those men. His writings will inspire and infuse you, help and bless you."
—**Thomas E. Trask**, Assemblies of God, Springfield, MO

"Edwin Louis Cole's resources are doing critical work on the frontline of spiritual warfare."
—**Ted Baehr,** Chairman,
The Christian Film and Television Commission

"Ed is an anointed man of God. His ministry is bringing America to a place of repentance and revival."
—**James Robison,** *Life Today*

"A nation rebels against the heavenly Father because it does not know what an earthly father is. Edwin Louis Cole is a role model for generations."
—**Doug Stringer**, Somebody Cares International

"This is a word for men today."
—**Mike Singletary**, NFL Hall-of-Famer

WHAT PEOPLE ARE SAYING ABOUT EDWIN LOUIS COLE...

"A whole new thrust is taking place with the resources developed by Ed Cole. I endorse these without reserve. I know what these materials do for men. Please accept my encouragement, and get after it!"

—**Jack Hayford,** Pastor,
The Foursquare Church, Los Angeles

"Dr. Cole was a man in touch with God and men. I highly, highly, highly recommend his books and curriculum. Let him do for you what he has done for me and for millions of others—lift you up and teach you how to walk like a godly person."

—**John C. Maxwell,** Founder, EQUIP, Atlanta

"Ed Cole had a passion for ministry which was unexcelled. I know of no one who had any more creative concepts to help men achieve their maximum potential before the Lord. Ed Cole's stirring message gives the practical advice men need for victorious living."

—**Pat Robertson,** Founder & CEO,
Christian Broadcasting Network

"The hour is late and the problems are massive. Dr. Cole's message is part of God's answer to the tough times we face."

—**Billy Joe Daugherty,** Pastor,
Victory Christian Center

"Ed Cole's message on Christlike manhood impacted my life and helped me present the Gospel in a way men would appreciate. Our church is packed in five locations with men every weekend as a result!"

—**Leon Fontaine,** Springs Church, Winnepeg

"Edwin Louis Cole is an example—an inspiration to men in a time that cries out for leaders with sound moral values."

—**Oliver North**, Lt. Colonel, U. S. Marine Corps (ret.)

"Ed Cole's ministry produces 'fruit that remains'—godliness, righteousness, holiness."

—**Jim Garlow,** Pastor, Skyline Wesleyan Church

MAXIMIZED
MANHOOD

A GUIDE TO FAMILY SURVIVAL

MAXIMIZED

MANHOOD

A GUIDE TO FAMILY SURVIVAL

Edwin Louis Cole

WHITAKER
HOUSE

MAXIMIZED MANHOOD
Revised Version

ISBN-13: 978-0-88368-655-3
ISBN-10: 0-88368-655-4
Printed in the United States of America
© 1982, 2001 by Edwin Louis Cole

Whitaker House
1030 Hunt Valley Circle
New Kensington, PA 15068
www.whitakerhouse.com

Library of Congress Cataloging-in-Publication Data

Cole, Edwin Louis.
  Maximized manhood : a guide to family survival / by Edwin Louis Cole.
     p.   cm.
  ISBN 0-88368-655-4 (pbk.)
  1. Christian men—Religious life. I. Title.
  BV4528.2 .C65 2001
  248.8'42—dc21
                                           00-012687

8 9 10 11 12 13 14 15 **UI** 16 15 14 13 12 11 10

DEDICATION

To my wife, Nancy, "The loveliest lady in the land." Her love for over fifty years has been a source of strength, wisdom, and character, and without her, I do not know where I would be. Thank you, Nancy, for that wonderful life you so freely gave to help me become the man and person I am today.

To Paul, Lois, and Joann, who forgave me all my errors over the years and stayed with me as a never-ending source of encouragement and blessing.

To the men in the book, such as Doyle, Alan, Jim, John, Ben, Jack, and others, who have taught me so much about being a real man, and have endured my trying to teach them by word and deed. Thanks, guys.

And thank you to the publishers, Bob Whitaker, Sr., and Bob Whitaker, Jr., who continue to believe in the message and maintain our friendship.

CONTENTS

FOREWORD BY BEN KINCHLOW

There is a very interesting phenomenon occurring in America. From birth to late teens, a child's overwhelming perception of authority figures is nearly 100% female, with an occasional male making a generally ineffectual appearance.

In the hospital, female nurses are responsible for almost every aspect of childcare. At home, mother is usually the dominant authority figure. And 90% of the teachers in grade school are—you got it—women. The first police person a child meets is more than likely a female crossing guard.

When a child goes to the movies, grocery store, department stores, fast-food restaurants, fancy sit-down restaurants, vacation Bible school, or Sunday school, who sells the tickets, takes the orders, collects the money, shows him where to sit, or tells him about God? (Except in many churches where a man preaches to a congregation consisting of mostly women.) Who tells you what to wear, to clean up your room; who spends the money and pays the bills? In other words, who's really in charge? Is it any wonder that today's young man is making every effort to demonstrate that he's a real man—like MOM.

So today's man may wear jewelry—bracelets, neck-laces, and, perhaps, an earring. He has long hair and wears tight shirts opened to display "cleavage." Or he may be a "macho man," who acts irresponsibly with his wife and children, or who indulges in sexual "freedom" and does his "own thing."

In any case, man is "liberated." Or so he's been told by feminist principles, which undercut his position as a male.

At the same time, women are wearing shorter haircuts, masculine pants and suits, and in some cases, neckties. In an attempt to "assert" their true selves or "punish their oppressors," many women have allowed suppressed rage or self-hatred to erupt into violence against the men they perceive as being at fault.

Men and women, not knowing exactly who they are or what their respective roles are, are confused and anxiety ridden.

There is a psychology called "muddling." Men often will not make a clear-cut decision on, or commitment to, anything; they just "muddle through." Since nature abhors a vacuum, women have been sucked into the areas that men have abandoned. As a result, men, women, and children are angry and frustrated and in increasing numbers are facing "identity crises."

Into the "middle of the muddle," like a stinging slap in the midst of hysteria, a gauntlet slammed down in challenge, or the shock of icy cold water, strides the ringing declaration of *Maximized Manhood*. This book contains not a mere rhetorical discussion, but a head-on confrontation with the issues.

This book is unabashedly, uncompromisingly, written to men. There are many books *about* us, but precious few written *to* us. It is a throwback to the days of man-to-man talks, male virtues, chivalry, and a respect for women and children that grew out of understanding the responsibility of being a "grown man." It is a book that enables us to discover the maximum potential of our lives to live as *maximized men*. It is long overdue.

Pungent and direct, this book challenges today's man. Some may be so angry at the assertions that they will want to slam the book down and quit. Others will be tempted to fire off a hot letter to "get Ed Cole straightened out."

Some men will read it, agree with some of its precepts and principles, but be unwilling to accept its calls for sacrifice. Without any real commitment to change, nothing will happen to them. Others, though they agree at the "gut level," will be intimidated by the "harsh realities of now" and find many of the book's positions challenged by today's popular trends. As a result, they will reject the truth in this book.

There are men, however, who will read this book, agree with it, and put its dynamic principles into practice. It will revolutionize their families, their wives, and their own lives. From there, it can even revolutionize the nation.

Genesis 1:27–30 says, *"God created man in His own image; in the image of God He created him; male and female He created them. Then God blessed them, and God said to them, 'Be fruitful and multiply; fill the earth and subdue it; have dominion....' And it was so."*

Being a male is a matter of birth; being a man is a matter of choice. Thank You, Lord, for making us who we are. Thank you, Ed, for reminding us.

PREFACE TO THE NEW EDITION

Millions of men have read this book since it was first published in 1982. When I was asked to update the content, I left it in its original form, except for minor editing I wished I had done before the first printing. In addition, I have added some chapters that not only validate what was written originally, but also give expanded revelation and deeper meaning to the truth that *"Manhood and Christlikeness are synonymous."*

CHAPTER 1

MAXIMUM SENTENCE

I was grateful United Airlines had a nonstop flight from Los Angeles to Eugene, Oregon. I was wearing four different hats at the time, juggling a variety of responsibilities and spending much of my life in airports and on airplanes. I was glad I wouldn't have to connect through Portland or Reno or some such place to get to Eugene for the retreat.

It was a men's retreat, the first of two that were scheduled on back-to-back weekends in the snowy mountains of west central Oregon. In between, I would dash up to Seattle and do another conference. Then, finally, a quick trip home to southern California, and I'd be off again somewhere.

Preaching and teaching, those lofty endeavors, were outlined in the aisle seats of so many jumbo jets. Much of my ministry preparation was done in that narrow slice of space between armrests aboard the aircraft.

Now, as United carried me toward Eugene, I tried to settle my mind into a studying mode.

Men.

There would be more than five hundred of them in the two retreats combined. I knew that they were gathering to hear something worthwhile, something life-changing, something they could take back to their homes and their offices, their shops, and their hunting trips. They wanted something that would help them reach the maximum in their manhood, enabling them to live more Christlike than ever.

The upcoming retreat was small in comparison with many events where I had ministered, or even in comparison with the television ministry in which I had been engaged for years. There was no reason why this trip should seem at all special.

> **They wanted something that would help them reach the maximum in their manhood.**

Yet there was a weightiness, a sobriety, a heaviness that would not go away. God was doing something in my spirit. I sensed that this jaunt to Oregon to speak to *men* was a major milestone in my life.

For weeks I had been praying for the right words to say. Pictures of modern man paraded across my mind. In our society, a moral pollution is taking its toll on manhood; it is disintegrating before our eyes. I began to realize what a great need there is for men to understand what is happening and to do something about it.

Things are not as God intended.

The jet engines whined in the background, and my Bible and notebook were both opened on the tray table in front of me. But in my meditation, I seemed to lose consciousness of my surroundings. Something was happening in my spirit. I was aware of the presence of God.

I recalled the teaching that Campbell McAlpine, a well-known Bible teacher, had brought to our fellowship of believers a few weeks before. The passage of Scripture he had used had a powerful impact on me. It was as though it were alive, and I had been dwelling on its importance for men ever since.

Campbell had spoken on 1 Corinthians 10. The sixth through ninth verses list the five reasons why the Israelites did not get into Canaan, the Land of Promise.

It was a basic truth—that God has a Land of Promise and blessing for His people. The Israelites had missed their opportunity to enter that land because of five basic sins.

But for me, this Scripture had a meaning that transcended anything I had ever thought of before. This chronicle of sins related to Israel, but there was a direct correlation to modern man. Scripture says the Israelites were examples for us.

> **God has a Land of Promise and blessing for His people.**

What did it mean for men today?

I looked down at my Bible. I reread the chapter in Corinthians, meditating on those five reasons for Israel's failure to reach the Promised Land.

The right words, right approach, right timing are so important to ministry. I wanted this message for these men on the snow-covered mountains of Oregon to be right.

Here were the reasons for failure, listed in the Word:

- Lust
- Idolatry
- Fornication
- Tempting Christ
- Murmuring

As I went through that list of sins that Campbell taught, the sin of fornication stood out. I began to think about people I had known—know even now—who failed to reach their Promised Land because of sex sins.

Couples, men, friends, preachers, congressmen, senators, people from every walk of life. Believers and non-believers. Sinners and saints.

A short time before, a friend of mine from California had approached me. "You know, Ed, you really need to get hot on the subject of sexual promiscuity," he told me point-blank, "because its happening all over Orange County! There are people living together and not married, and still going to church and believing they're Christians!"

The children of Israel had nothing on us. We match sin for sin.

Something happened at a family breakfast one morning that really jolted me. As we sat around the breakfast table, I mentioned to my wife, Nancy, and my daughter, Joann, about my growing concern for the sexual problems of modern man.

They listened quietly to me, and then Joann responded with an insight from both her college life and her Christian understanding.

"Dad, don't you know that sex sins will be the problem of the church in the '80s?"

I just looked at her. It had never occurred to me just that way. But after she said it, like a light springing up within me, I saw an instant picture of our national life—men and women, young and old, leaders and common people alike—all across America. Then around the world. I saw it.

It had been evident that the moral fiber of our nation was being weakened and even shredded on every hand. But then I saw that the church was not immune.

The mores of society were imposing themselves on the church of Jesus Christ.

So many lives—all being affected by sex sins.

Campbell's teaching, Joann's word of wisdom. God's Word.

With United Airlines bringing me closer to my destination, and moment by moment nearer to my appointment, I suddenly began to write. I was aware that God's Spirit within me was inspiring me and guiding that pen as I wrote on the page in my notebook.

The mores of society were imposing themselves on the church.

Finished, I looked at what I had written.

The sentence was one I had never seen before—not like that—nor had I ever said anything like it.

A sentence of such pungency that I stared at it for a long time, wondering when, where, or to whom it would be given. My spirit suddenly leaped within me, for I knew it was for that night, those men, that retreat.

It was too powerful for me, too bold—even for a prophet-preacher like myself, who had preached to large crowds. But nothing like this.

This was God.

I knew I would have to say it.

When? How?

Timing is everything in a situation like this.

I would have to declare it. Command it.

Aloud. Publicly. With authority.

And—that night—to those men at Camp Davidson, on the mountainous outskirts of Eugene, Oregon.

Without God's power, it could be terrible—with God's confirmation and vindication, it could be glorious. Bringing liberty.

It was for me to say. For me to command.

For God to vindicate.

CHAPTER 2

KEPT OUT OF CANAAN

That evening in Oregon, in the meeting tucked away in a rustic chapel among pine trees, it came my turn to speak. I knew exactly what to do and what to say. There was no doubt. No indecision.

As I stood before the unsuspecting crowd of men, I felt an accelerating sense of excitement. I had them stand with me as I led them through a confession of Jesus Christ and His Lordship, and then in a prayer of agreement, as I always do before ministering.

Then, before they could sit down, I looked them in the eye and gave them God's command:

> If you are here tonight and committing adultery, fornication, homosexuality, incest, or habitual masturbation; indulging in pornography; gratifying yourself with sexual fantasies or any other kind of sex sin, I command you in the name of Jesus Christ of Nazareth to repent and be restored to a right relationship with God the Father by being reconciled through Jesus Christ and the power of the Holy Spirit.

The room fell silent for a split second. Those words, so awkwardly scribbled on a simple notepad a few hours before, now cut through the air like an electric shock. With a single explosive motion, the men's hands shot into the air, and they began crying out in praise and worship to God. The Holy Spirit filled that chapel in the mountains, bringing a remarkable response to a savagely honest question.

These men—businessmen, preachers, laborers, young and old—had craved direction. They had longed for leadership. They had sought God's voice—no matter how stern.

> **Canaan Land has always been God's symbol of mankind's maximized potential.**

They had been crying out for a change in their lives, an end to questionings and wanderings. Like the hapless children of Israel, men today dream of a Promised Land, a Canaan. It is a life where problems can be solved, conflicts ended, and relationships renewed. A life of strength and sustenance.

They longed for a Canaan Land.

Now, right here, let me explain to you the meaning of Canaan Land and how it applies to your life.

Canaan Land has always been God's symbol of mankind's maximized potential. Canaan is the place where God's promises are fulfilled in our lives—the place where God maximizes the potential of His people both individually and collectively. And it affects their spirits, emotions, and bodies; their marriages, children, and professions.

In the Old Testament, Canaan Land was where God wanted the Israelites to live after He delivered them from their bondage in Egypt. They were to live there in faith, and God would fulfill His promises to them.

22

I want you to understand that Canaan is a Land of Promise where God wants you to live by faith today. There, He will fulfill His promises in your life. There, you can reach your maximum potential.

Shangri–la was a fantasy; Canaan Land is real.

But the Israelites failed to reach Canaan.

They failed for those five basic reasons that are listed in 1 Corinthians 10.

Those five reasons are the same reasons why men today do not get their Canaan Land fulfillment in life. God wants men to have Canaan Land marriages, businesses, parental relationships, educations.

Yet men are not maximized in their marriages, businesses, or relationships.

Men with unfulfilled potential.

That may be you, or someone you know.

Those five basic sins still plague men today and keep them from the fulfillment of potential in their lives.

Here are the big five!

LUST

Now this lust is not necessarily sexual lust—that comes later when we deal with sex sins. This is the lust that is based on satisfying self at the expense of God and others. It's the preoccupation with what self wants. This is the satisfaction or gratification of the flesh.

> **Love is of God, and true love is always giving.**

Love is of God, and true love is always giving. God's love desires to satisfy the object of His love. *"For God so loved the world that He gave His only begotten Son"* (John 3:16). God is love. Love gives.

But lust wants to get. It is basically selfish.

Love gives; lust gets. The entire direction of life differs between the two. The Israelites craved what they had in Egypt. Their feet were taking them to Canaan, but their hearts kept going back to Egypt.

They were lovers of pleasure more than lovers of God.

You can tell today when men or women are lusting. They desire to satisfy themselves at the expense of others. By the same token, you can tell when they are loving, because they desire to satisfy their loved ones at the expense of themselves.

Love gives; lust gets.

A man may be married but lust after his wife sexually when he cares only about satisfying himself and leaves her unfulfilled and unsatisfied. It's obvious that the young man professing love for the girl is only lusting when he satisfies himself sexually and leaves her to face pregnancy alone and fearful.

Or a woman is lusting when she uses the credit cards to run up bills that her husband cannot pay, creating a terrible hardship on the family. Professing love, she is really lusting.

Corporations lust, one against the other. Even nations lust against each other.

But by now, you can make up your own list of the way people either love or lust. Lust today keeps men (and women) from maximizing their potential.

IDOLATRY

Idolatry is a value system that we create, in which we esteem something to be more worthy of our devotion than devotion to God.

Power, prestige, education, money, business, religion, popularity, ego, pornography—can all become idols.

Some men worship at the shrine of their businesses; others at temples of recreation and sports. Still others may bow at the sound of the cash register.

For some ministers, even their ministry can become an idol. They become so devoted to it that they cannot take time to worship God, wait in His presence, or spend time ministering to Him.

For others, their television set has become an idol.

All pornography is idolatrous. It's based on man's ability to create in his mind a fantasy or image that satisfies him, and to which he can devote himself.

I was in Phoenix and mentioned this one evening. A woman there told me that the soap operas on television had become so powerful to her that she started a fantasy sex life that sometimes would occupy her for several hours. After which, she was so weak she could not make supper for her husband. She said it was worse than alcoholism to her.

> **Idolatry is man's ability to create in his mind an image to which he can devote himself.**

Corporate life in America today has become idolatrous in many instances. Men sacrifice their families for the sake of the company.

Many actors worship themselves. Anyone can do that, but more of them are susceptible to it because of the adoration that fans show them.

Idolatry keeps men from being maximized in their potential—personally, maritally, professionally, spiritually.

FORNICATION

Actually, this sin includes every kind of sex sin.

Sin is still sin, no matter how you spell it.

Fornication is popular and sexual promiscuity is acceptable everywhere today—except in the Bible. No wonder men want to burn it, deny it, or crucify it. The Word still sets the standard of faith, gives the rule of conduct, and reveals the character of God.

Reading about Samson, David, and others in Scripture is in itself a vital lesson concerning the results of sex sins. But the roll call goes on today. Man after man, who in many areas of life develops the potential of his manhood, is limited because of his sex sins.

> **God's promise to sit with Him on His throne is given to those who are called overcomers.**

Both single and married men, young and old, are subject to the desires, appetites, passions, and temptations that take their toll and prohibit them from becoming what God intends them to be.

Men's ministries are undeveloped or lost.

Men's characters are underdeveloped or weak.

God's promise to sit with Him on His throne is given to those who are called overcomers. Overcomers are godly achievers. Every man is given opportunity to enter his Canaan, to develop his potential of manhood to the maximum.

When the men of Israel committed fornication, they died in the wilderness, never seeing Canaan. Men still die in their wildernesses, bogged down in a moral morass, missing God's best for their lives.

It wasn't God's plan then or now.

TEMPTING CHRIST

When the crowds demanded that Christ come down from the cross, they tempted Him. Tempting Christ is demanding that God do what is contrary to His will or inconsistent with His character. Today, men still do the same by demanding that God provide some way of salvation other than the Cross.

Lying and cheating in business and demanding that God bless and prosper the results is tempting Christ. Men and women pursuing promiscuity, though they know it is wrong; children rejecting the godly counsel of parents; congregations demanding the pastor build the church on social programs rather than the Word of God and prayer; believers wanting to enjoy the benefits of salvation and the pleasures of sin at the same time—all are tempting Christ.

> **Tempting Christ means demanding that God do what is contrary to His character.**

It kept Israel from Canaan.

It keeps men from their Canaan today.

MURMURING

Murmuring in its simplest form is nothing more or less than "negative confession."

Complaining, criticizing, faultfinding, rumoring—all and more are classified as murmuring. First Corinthians 5:11 KJV speaks of a *"railer,"* a word we don't ordinarily use today. A railer is a slanderer, a blasphemer, a reviler, and God requires us to deal with them in vehemence and discipline.

27

"How great a matter a little fire kindleth!" (James 3:5 KJV).

The tongue is like that. Small remarks, cutting comments, or sarcastic jibes eventually create roaring bonfires of hate, warfare, and enmity. Consuming relationships, it leaves nothing but embers.

Men murmur about their company or boss at the water cooler, and then complain because they do not get promoted. They murmur against the preacher, and wonder why their children don't respond to the Gospel. They murmur against God's Word, and then complain when they don't see faith take effect in their lives.

No Canaan there.

When I saw these five sins, it became glaringly apparent that they are still the five root causes for men living in unfulfilled potential. They are basic to all humanity.

> **It is obvious that men are never becoming all that God intended them to be.**

God wants men to enter into Canaan—that place of rest, blessing, success, ability, and authority—where He desires them to be. However, it is obvious that men are still wandering in a wilderness, dying because of sin. Never becoming all that God intended them to be.

Five basic sins.

The sentence God gave me on that plane flying to the Oregon retreat was directed specifically at one of those sins: fornication.

It was powerful and had a phenomenal result.

Two hundred and sixty-five men ran toward the front of that chapel and began to repent of their sins with an earnest desire to be fulfilled in their potential as men of God. Some wept aloud.

Wall to wall, men standing before God. So great was the power of God that night—not one man went away untouched or unchanged.

As you read this, I make the same command to you. If you are bound by any of those sex sins in your life, make this the place for repentance and restoration. Let God do the same thing in you at this very moment that He did in the hearts of those men that night. God wants you to be the person you've always wanted to be.

Be a man. (Or woman, if you are reading this.)

Those men were just like you—same desires, questions, problems—same reasons for unfulfilled potential.

That night I was ecstatic. I saw God's power change men and literally saw them grow in spirit before my very eyes. It was incredibly great.

But later, I ached for the millions of others. I knew that the troubles of twentieth-century man were not limited to this tiny group, nor to the next group to whom I would speak.

I knew countless other men would never find their way to a retreat, a church service, a fellowship meeting, or a conference. And even as I prayed with those men in that little chapel in Oregon, I felt the Holy Spirit prompt me to move out. To declare God's commands across the nation, to both believing and non-believing men everywhere, in their towns, cities, and communities.

It was mind-boggling.

Yet I knew God had prepared me for precisely this.

CHAPTER 3

THE *PLAYBOY* PROBLEM

I have a problem," the young lady said, a little shyly. It was the close of a noon prayer meeting for the employees of a large East Coast ministry. I had just concluded a brief Bible study and dismissed the meeting when the girl drew me to one side for private prayer.

"What is your problem?" I asked.

"I have a problem," she repeated obliquely.

"Yes," I replied, wondering if she had heard me correctly. "Exactly what can I agree with you in prayer concerning?"

Her face drew tight, and tears welled up in her eyes.

"I don't really know," she stammered, biting her lip, "but I have a real problem."

I tried to be firm without being harsh. "Ours is a God of specifics, not generalities," I told her. "I will be happy to pray with you, but I need to know the nature of your problem so that I can pray specifically. Nobody else will know, just you and me."

"Well, I really don't know what my problem is," she responded in a halting fashion. "But my husband says I have a problem."

I tried again. "What does your husband say your problem is?"

"He says I don't understand him," she finally said, agonizing over each word.

"What don't you understand?" I asked.

Suddenly, the girl began to weep, bitterly, from deep within.

"My husband keeps magazines by his side of the bed," she gasped quietly between sobs. "*Playboy, Penthouse,* and those other magazines. He says he needs to look at them before he can have sex with me. He says he needs them to stimulate himself."

She squeezed out the sentence, tears flowing down her face.

"I told him he doesn't really need those magazines, but he says I don't understand him. He says if I really loved him, then I would understand why he has to have the magazines, and I would let him get more of them."

"What does your husband do for a living?" I inquired.

"He's a youth minister."

I stood there, incredulous, as I realized what she was telling me. I was listening to this woman tell me that her husband was a youth minister who kept a pile of pornographic literature by his bed!

"Your husband may be a youth minister," I responded evenly, "but he is also a pornographer."

The girl's head snapped to attention. It was as if I had slapped her solidly across the face. She had never expected to hear her husband described as a pornographer. And yet, his lifestyle made him exactly that.

In this modern era, we don't have sins. We have problems. We have psychologized the Gospel, and in the process, we have eliminated the word *sin* from our vocabulary.

THE *PLAYBOY* PROBLEM

A woman came to me once with a sad story. Her husband had treated her badly for years and had finally left her, suing for divorce. A church member, a confessed Christian for many years, she now found herself alone—and lonely.

Responding to her feelings, she went to a nearby city and spent the weekend with a man. She had, as she put it, "biological necessities."

"Do you realize what you have done?" I demanded as she sat in my office.

The lady was taken aback. "Why, what are you talking about?"

"You are an adulteress," I said.

Her eyes opened wide, and her face flushed with shock. She was offended that I had called her an adulteress.

> **In this modern era, we have eliminated the word *sin* from our vocabulary.**

And yet, having committed adultery, she was an adulteress.

To her it had not been a sin—just a problem she had.

We don't talk about sins today; we talk about problems. Problems are more convenient than sins because we don't have to do anything about problems. If you only have a problem, you can get sympathy for it or understanding for it or professional help for it, to name a few. Sins, on the other hand, have to be repented, confessed, and forsaken.

No wonder Freud wanted to get rid of the word *sin*.

In the process of rewriting biblical language, we have escaped a confrontation with our sins. But without that confrontation, we don't do anything about them.

All problems in life are somehow based on sin. That is why man needs a Savior from his sins as an answer to his problems. God knew that. That's why Jesus Christ came to die for our sins and be the answer to all our problems.

Church discipline is lax, weak, or nonexistent in many churches. The apostle Paul advocated discipline.

If anyone calls himself a brother, Paul wrote, and maintains a lifestyle or habitual pattern of sin, don't keep company with him; don't even have lunch with him.

Have no fellowship!

> **Man needs a Savior from his sins. Jesus came to die for our sins and answer all our problems.**

"But now I have written unto you not to keep company, if any man that is called a brother be a fornicator, or covetous, or an idolater, or a railer, or a drunkard, or an extortioner; with such an one no not to eat" (1 Corinthians 5:11 KJV).

Contrary to what you, or anyone else, may think, this is an act of love, not of hate. You see, God's ways are as high above our ways as the heavens are above the earth.

Paul had the mind of the Lord when he wrote those words. If a person calling himself a Christian continues in his sin with impunity and is allowed full membership privileges, he has no incentive to confront and confess and set aside his sin. Why should there be any change? The person has the sin and still has the acceptance of the believers.

Often, the person committing the sin would rather admit that he has a problem, or that he is just unfortunate, and will wail or cry when dealt with in discipline.

Human sorrow is when we are only sorry for getting caught. Godly sorrow is when we are sorry for the sin and have a desire to be rid of it.

If Paul were living in our day, he would be contesting the modern secular humanists, laying siege to the strongholds of thought that have taken hold of our minds and blinded us to the truth. There really are seducing spirits and doctrines of devils. We see them at work in our world today. We have been seduced into thinking we have problems instead of sins. Our modern doctrines, stemming

> **Godly sorrow is when we are sorry for the sin and have a desire to be rid of it.**

from lives devoid of God's life, tell us, "I'm all right, and you're all right," rather than, *"All have sinned, and come short of the glory of God"* (Romans 3:23 KJV).

I went out for coffee with an embattled pastor. He had nearly lost his church.

Choir members of the congregation had known for a long time that the minister of music had committed acts of homosexuality. He had been involved to the extent that it was known openly.

For a long time, nobody said a word. They were all hoping that something would happen and a change would occur. Finally, the secret leaked out and eventually was told to the pastor. After much prayer and diligent searching out of the truth, the time came when the pastor and music minister met and confronted the issue. The music minister admitted everything.

"You need to do one of two things," the pastor told him directly. "You must either repent or resign."

The music minister considered the choices and made his calculated decision. He would do neither. Instead, he began to circulate among the choir members, and then among the other people in the congregation, currying favors.

Presently, a delegation of choir members approached the pastor.

"You don't understand," the spokesman offered. "He simply has a problem. If we just surround him with love and understanding, that will help him, and he will be able to change."

"You don't understand," the pastor replied. "If you simply surround him with love and understanding, and he doesn't have to repent of his sin, he will *never* be able to change."

The battle lines were drawn. The delegation spread out into the church, fanning the fires and turning other church members against the godly pastor, whom they accused of being unloving. Uproar ensued. A furious meeting was held, and by divine intervention, the godly pastor stayed.

The music minister left, together with many sympathizers. The church went through a difficult period of time, but God vindicated that godly pastor's position. Today that church is stronger than it was before the crisis. The pastor himself is a stronger man.

> **Human wisdom has mangled the gospel truth.**

Human wisdom has mangled the gospel truth.

The difference between human wisdom and divine wisdom, when it comes to sin, is that human wisdom wants to cover it up. Adam tried to do that in the Garden. First, it was symbolic, as he covered his nakedness. Then, it was more than symbolic, as he started the process of self-justification, by placing his guilt and failure on Eve in order to cover his sin.

Cover yourself; blame somebody.

THE *PLAYBOY* PROBLEM

That faulty human wisdom is still at work today. Watergate became the classic modern example of cover-up. The weary, yet resolute, pastor refused to allow human wisdom and mere sentimentality to stand in the way of divine rightness. He would not allow sin to be covered up and called "a problem." Behavioral psychology has no textbook adequate to deal with the scope of human dilemma. God wrote the Book on salvation from sin long before it became "problem solving."

God commands obedience to His Word. He does not allow the fashionable when it violates His sovereign Word. Our modern laissez-faire attitude is not cute to God. It is an abomination to Him, and He commands us—not invites, but commands us—to repent and obey.

> **God commands us—not invites, but commands us—to repent and obey.**

The gap between human wisdom and divine wisdom is immeasurably wide. In our fleshly wisdom we have reordered our value system according to our lusts. Man looks at his space technology, Neiman Marcus suits, a pithy *Time* magazine, and thinks he is wise. He teaches or is taught philosophies that can only provide questions but no answers. He espouses a science that mocks Creation, yet is unable to provide anything but an unproven theory for what he believes about evolution.

"Who is wise and understanding among you?" James 3:13 asks pointedly. *"If you have bitter envy and self-seeking in your hearts, do not boast and lie against the truth"* (verse 14).

Our troubled world, filled with envy, strife, and difficulty, is the product of our own proud, worldly wisdom.

Human wisdom taught a generation of world leaders to believe that the deeper your debt, the better off the economy will be. This philosophy has brought America to the brink of economic ruin.

The sophisticated spirit of the modern era based on human wisdom brings discord, hurt, and eventual ruin.

It is true that since Eden, man has not improved in his nature. He may have more technical knowledge, but his nature is still the same. Saying that humanity is improved because of man's technical expertise is like saying a cannibal is better because he has a knife and fork.

> **You can never maximize your potential until you have received God's wisdom.**

"But the wisdom that is from above," James concluded, *"is first pure, then peaceable, gentle, willing to yield, full of mercy and good fruits, without partiality and without hypocrisy"* (James 3:17). That is divine wisdom.

The human wisdom that sends us out to do our own thing is not the wisdom that will lead us into Canaan Land. You can never maximize your potential until you have received God's wisdom.

Tough, but true.

The sweethearts living together out of wedlock are really fornicators.

The foul-mouthed teenager is really a railer.

God is no semantic masseur. He talks a man's language. Scripture lays it on the line: sin is sin.

Talk is not cheap. It cost Jesus Christ His life for the Gospel to be preached. Such talk has eternal consequences.

In Texas I heard a story of a Texan who died and went to his eternal reward. Once inside the gate, he stood there, taking it all in. The host came to escort him to his eternal abode.

The Texan turned to the host and said, "Pardner, I didn't realize heaven was so much like Texas."

The host turned back and replied, "Man, you aren't in heaven."

That back-slapping story has a chilling point. There will be no sudden answers when the "problem person" plunges into a Christless eternity.

Sins will be taken seriously then, but too late.

The "*Playboy* syndrome," "biological necessities," and homosexual "problems" will be no more.

We must begin to tackle sin like men.

CHAPTER 4

MOSES AND THE
TEN INVITATIONS

I like men. I like a man's man," I told the congregation. "I like men of worth, value, character. I like real men."

We were in a meeting in southern California years ago, and even then I had a vital interest in manhood and character development. I was speaking to a large audience of both men and women.

"I don't like the pussyfooting pipsqueaks who tippy toe through the tulips," I said in my most eloquent manner. "I like men to be men."

Suddenly, I remembered that much of that congregation was female, so I sheepishly shrugged and apologized, "I'm sorry, ladies. I can't help it. I like men."

A little gray-haired lady in the center of the crowd leaped briskly to her feet and shouted, "Amen, brother. I like them, too!"

The place exploded with laughter.

Unfortunately, the affection that men and women have for each other can take a variety of forms. What each may like in a general sense at the altar, they may find unlikable when the pressures of life come.

Pressure magnifies problems.

The modern method is to say goodbye when the pressure mounts. The modern trend is to escape, to shrug at scriptural imperatives, and say, "Better luck next time."

I can recall years ago when Dr. Leland Keys spoke about the easy dissolution of marriage in our society. A Christian couple, he said, were suing for divorce based on incompatibility: he lost his income and she lost her "patability."

But God's commandments are absolutes.

God commands us to love.

Our modern age mistakes lust for love; it relegates love to a glandular function, a reaction to the angle of a neckline or the height of a skirt. Not all of passion is love and not all of love is passion.

> **God commands us to love. His commandments are absolutes.**

According to God, love is not a feeling. Sometimes it doesn't even *feel* good. But real love is always good.

Love centers in the will. That is why love can be commanded and why God can command love.

The American male, to a great extent today, flees from commandments. Or rebels. Numberless times I have listened to either men or women tell me of their inability to love, saying, "I can't love anymore. I just can't feel anything." Not true!

God commands us to love. And He gives us the ways to accomplish it. His ways.

When God's love is placed in our hearts by the Holy Spirit, real love is known. By yielding your will to the will of God, and allowing the Holy Spirit to bring God's love into your relationship, you can love. Why? Because God commands it.

I was standing in front of a table at the end of a meeting when an exuberant couple greeted me. With their arms interlocked and occasionally smiling at each other, they told me of the miracle in their lives.

"If you ever want anyone to confirm what you said about God giving love, just call us," the husband said. "We are a miracle marriage. For years I made my wife's life a hell on earth. Unfaithful, inconsiderate, dictatorial, selfish—all I wanted was for her to do what was necessary for me to enjoy life.

"Oh, I led the choir, we went to church, and everyone saw us as a fine family, but no one knew me privately. Not even she did. I was a first-rate hypocrite for years.

"All she knew was that she had come to the end of her rope and was leaving me. That's when I awoke to how and what I was.

"Then, I changed. Or rather, the Lord Jesus Christ changed me. When I confessed what I was and how I was living, and genuinely repented with godly sorrow, God heard my prayer and changed me.

"But by then, my wife didn't want me. She said whatever love she had was dead, and she could never love me again. I knew she believed that, but I was believing in a God of miracles. So I prayed and began to love her in my heart, and to court her as I had at the first. Only this time, the Lord helped me. Eventually, she agreed to try the marriage again, because divorce was against everything she believed.

"Together we began to pray and talk—and I loved her. You know, today we love each other as we never did before. I have such a genuine appreciation for God. He really can make what was dead live again. You tell the world that if God did it for us, He can do it for them."

That was in a men's meeting in Thousand Oaks, California. That couple is still in the area, and they are telling everyone who will listen that God is a God of the miraculous!

God commands us to repent.

> **God is a God of the miraculous!**

I was a guest on a local Christian talk show some time ago. During the show, I was explaining to the host and cohost that the Lord had impressed me to *command* men to repent.

There was a pause for a station break. The cohost leaned toward me and, with our microphones dead, said, "No, no, no! We *command* Christians, but *invite* sinners."

"No, no, no," I responded. "Acts 17:30 says, *'These times of ignorance God overlooked, but now commands all men everywhere to repent.'* There is a key difference between a *command* and an *invitation.*"

If I give you an invitation, you have an option. You can either receive it or reject it. But if I command you, you have no option. You either obey or rebel.

God didn't take Moses up on the mountain and give him a list of "Ten Invitations." God gave *commandments*.

In the psychologizing of the Gospel in the modern pulpit, we have been taught to "invite" people to accept Jesus. Given the option, they reject it.

It's like the bumper sticker that says, "Try Jesus."

That's like saying, "Try it; you'll like it." You may say that with peanut butter, asparagus, or spinach—but not with God. God doesn't command anyone to "like" him. God says "love."

What an arrogant attitude. It's as if they were really saying, "I'll try this Savior Jesus, and if I don't like Him,

I'll try another savior." Or, "I'll try this marriage, and if it doesn't work, I'll try another." As if either God or marriage can be tried on like a new suit or dress. What gall! How nauseous!

Who do such people think God is? Some doddering old deity sitting on the front porch of a celestial shack, rocking away the eons, letting the world do "wheelies" around the sun?

God is all-powerful, all-knowing, all-seeing.

God created this whole thing, including you and me, and by His active presence, He sustains it all. God is all-powerful, all-knowing, all-seeing.

We are not *invited* to obey God.

We are *commanded* to obey.

By Him.

The Holy Spirit doesn't come sidling up to some person and ask, "Will you please obey Me today?"

When a man obeys God, he maximizes his manhood.

God maximizes a man's personality, talent, and character.

Satan is a usurper. He comes only to steal, kill, and destroy. Satan and sin will rob you of your personality; you can see it in every addict. Satan will steal your character; God will maximize it. Satan plunders; God empowers and ennobles.

Obedience to God's commands brings peace.

Peace is heavenly. Only obedience can bring peace. Disobedience shatters the peace. That's why no disobedient spirit will ever get to heaven. Just one person with a disobedient spirit, and the peace would be broken. There was one—Lucifer. God expelled him. There will never be another. Not Lucifer, not you, not anyone.

Obedience to God's commands brings peace.

Two of my dearest friends live in California. Steve and his wife, Gail, are precious. Their home is peaceful, joyous, and filled with love. It wasn't always that way, though.

I became acquainted with Steve when he and his best friend came to my door to sell insurance. Instead, we talked of the blessings of the Lord Jesus. As a result, they began to attend the church I was pastoring many years ago.

During one daughter's serious illness, Steve prayed and saw her healed. From then until now he has had a deep abiding love for God—all except once. That time almost cost him his marriage, family, profession—and soul.

Steve worked in an office where flirtation among the office force was a daily ritual. The women working there seemed to expect it, and the men fulfilled their expectations. But Steve became more than flirtatious. What started as flirtation became dating, then petting, and finally adultery.

Unable to live with his conscience, he made the decision to leave his wife and family, and live the sensuous, glamorous life. He moved into an apartment, and his girlfriend moved in with him.

"Stolen water is sweet, and bread eaten in secret is pleasant, but he does not know that the dead are there, that her guests are in the depths of hell," it says in Proverbs 9:17–18.

Steve lost his peace of heart.

Gail and her daughters were devastated. Long nights followed—nights of tearful introspection of what went wrong, where the mistakes had been made, how it could have happened. No peace. Not in him, her, the girls, or anywhere.

Disobedience brought confusion, pain, and suffering. It dispelled all peace.

But Gail knew God. She trusted God's Word. Her faith was unshakable. Indefatigable. So during those agonizing days, she spent hours in counseling and prayer. She looked into God's Word, not only to find His promise for Steve's recovery, but also for the changes necessary in her so she could love, forgive, and find reconciliation. She was a real woman.

The day came when Steve was arrested for drunk driving. In jail, Steve came to himself, like the Prodigal Son Jesus talked about. With deep contrition of heart and genuine sorrow for his sin, Steve cried from his heart and his cell.

God heard that cry, and He forgave Steve. Upon discharge, Steve went to his wife to ask forgiveness and to be restored to his home—and his bed. It was not easy for either of them. They both had to talk and pray through his guilt and her jealousy, but they did it. And their home was filled with the peace of God.

In their home today, it is as if it had never happened. That is why I changed their names in this story. I still visit them, love them, and appreciate being around them.

And, oh, yes, you would be surprised at the number of people they have helped, encouraged, and brought to reconciliation.

God commands confession.

God commands confession to get rid of sin, and confession to put on righteousness. Repentance from sin and faith toward God is the balance.

Unconfessed sin is unforgiven sin.

Sin can only come out of the life through the mouth.

My friend Campbell McAlpine said that and its truth has stuck with me.

In dealing with men in the rallies and seminars, I have also found that it is important that they know that forgiveness is not enough; there needs to be cleansing, too.

"If we confess our sins, He is faithful and just to forgive us our sins and to cleanse us from all unrighteousness" (1 John 1:9).

So often I have seen men repent of sin and feel a real sense of forgiveness. They leave the place of prayer satisfied with their spiritual condition—only to find themselves repeating the same sin, and then needing the same forgiveness. God's way is to forgive us, then cleanse us so we won't continue in the habitual pattern of besetting sin. We are freed from it.

> **God's way is to forgive us, then cleanse us so we won't continue in sin.**

People are looking for truth. They're looking for reality.

Deal with people in truth, and you deal with reality. Speaking the truth isn't even enough, though. Truth must be spoken in love.

I've met scores of people who think they are doing right by being very outspoken. Then, they put a veneer of respectability on what they say by commenting, "Well, I believe in telling the truth. You will always know what I think." Sometimes I want to say, "Who cares?" Most of those kinds of people may speak the truth, but more often than not, it is not spoken in love.

On the other hand, some people are afraid of the truth. They are afraid of hurting others or of losing their love. They don't realize that truth, spoken in love, is the only way to show real love.

I call this kind of backward loving—*best affections.*

Let me illustrate.

If I am preaching and someone hands me a note in the middle of the sermon, and the note says that a member's house is burning down—at that very moment—what should I do? That person is in danger of losing everything. But if I interrupt my sermon and tell him about it, I am going to upset him and possibly make him feel bad. It might even hurt him. Because I do not want him to be distressed, hurt, or upset, I withhold the information.

Later, after church, the frantic parishioner comes crying, "My house burned down!"

"Yes," I respond. "I know."

The harried parishioner looks wide-eyed at me. "You know?"

"Sure," I state. "Remember the note that was handed to me in the middle of the sermon? It said your house was on fire."

"Why didn't you tell me?"

And my simple reply—"I didn't want to tell you because I knew it would make you feel bad."

Ridiculous. Yet we see it being done every day.

> **Speaking the truth isn't enough. Truth must be spoken in love.**

The mother who wants the best for her child, yet ruins the child by means of best affections. Stage mothers are like that. Also mothers-in-law try to help their children, but can destroy their marriages by means of best affections.

Pastors love their congregations. But they can be so solicitous and careful not to let anything happen without their approval that they destroy their churches by means of best affections.

How utterly stupid! Yet how many people are going without hearing the Word of God because someone doesn't want to make them feel bad, or cause them to be upset by talking about sin and hell?

I shall never forget when this was brought home to me so forcefully.

It was in the Bay Area of Texas. The pastor with whom I was ministering took me to visit the home of a woman who was dying of cancer. Her husband was a riverboat captain, a huge man, an intimidating physical presence. He took a leave of absence, borrowed money, and spent all his time at his wife's side ministering to her with tenderness, love, and compassion. He stayed with her night and day, devoted because of his great love for this frail bit of a woman.

The pastor wanted me to go with him in the hopes that we would be able to speak to the woman about the condition of her soul, and her relationship with God. Many years before, she had been very active in the church, but through a misunderstanding, her feelings had been hurt. She developed a bitter spirit toward the church and never went again. The pastor was very concerned that before anything else happened, she would have an opportunity to confess Jesus Christ again and be assured of her eternity in the presence of God.

In her living room, she sat in a wheelchair, weakened, ravaged, odorous, but making every effort to converse and be hospitable, even in her condition. We had talked for only a few minutes, but I could tell by looking at her that she wanted one of us to talk to her about Jesus. She was hungry in her spirit. As I began to talk, her six-foot-six-inch tall husband put his huge ham-like hand ever so gently and deferentially on her shoulder, and said to me with cold finality, "She's a good woman. She's a precious woman. She loves God, and God loves her. She's done a lot of good for that there church, and God knows all she's done."

He would not let me lead her into a confession of faith toward Jesus because he did not want her to have to face the repentance for her sin. Destroying by means of best affections.

Remember, godly sorrow is necessary for repentance. Human sorrow is because you were caught, but godly sorrow is for the cause.

Sorrow is one of life's greatest teachers.

"No chastening seems to be joyful for the present, but painful; nevertheless, afterward it yields the peaceable fruit of righteousness to those who have been trained by it" (Hebrews 12:11).

It's what comes afterward that makes it all worthwhile.

The good news is that God never stops loving us.

A Sunday school teacher once asked her pupils, "Does God love you if you are a thief or a liar?" The children all answered, "No!" Wrong. God loves thieves, liars, cheats, murderers, addicts, and pimps, the pompous, proud, and arrogant. God loves the sinner, even though He hates the sin.

The good news is that God never stops loving us. God never stops loving. Period.

His entire purpose at Calvary was to be able to separate us from our sins. His wrath must be visited upon sin. As long as we are identified with sin, we are subject to His wrath. But by the new birth, we become identified with Jesus Christ and His righteousness; therefore, we are no longer under wrath but grace.

When God's Spirit brings conviction of sin to us, it is not to hurt us, even though it produces sorrow in us. It's to cause us to be willing to be separated from sin and its ugliness, so that God can bring His love, grace, and power into our lives in greater degree and measure.

God never stops loving. Period.

When I was just a boy and my mother was attending a Bible school in Los Angeles, I went with her and the other students to the skid row area where they preached the Gospel. Mom, Annie, Erdine, and all the others took their guitars, tambourines, and big bass drum. There on the street corner, playing and singing and preaching, they ministered to the worst of society, and the worst of the worst.

Early one evening, everyone was singing that grand old gospel song: "What can wash away my sin? Nothing but the blood of Jesus!"

A nondescript, unkempt, unclean alcoholic edged up close to Annie. People on skid row called them "winos." He was just like so many others, the stub of a wrinkled cigarette held between his yellowed fingers and dirty nails, his eyes glassy and filmed, his skin caked with dirt, and his clothes bagging, while he reeked with the smell of cheap wine.

Man whitewashes. God washes white.

He tugged at Annie's arm, and she pulled away. Several times he did that, until at last she turned toward him so he could speak to her while the others continued to sing.

"I know what you're saying is right," he said, his words slurred and slow, awkward and raspy. "Nothing but the blood of Jesus can wash away my sins."

I stood there, listening, watching, and impressed.

"I used to be the president of a seminary," he went on. "I know all about it. But you know, *there's a big, big difference between being washed white and being whitewashed.*"

Then he staggered away, while his words stayed behind, standing before me in my memory to this day.

He had been whitewashed.

Unconfessed sin is unforgiven sin.

Human wisdom covers up. Godly wisdom uncovers.

Man whitewashes. God washes white.

CHAPTER 5

THERE'S A HOLE IN THE DOOR

My son, Paul, had a new driver's license in his wallet. I came home for a day or two in the midst of all my ministerial travels, and Paul asked me that question that all dads "love" to hear.

"Can I have the car?" he queried.

"Why?" I asked.

"I want to go to youth camp at Mt. Lassen."

I had a mental file drawer full of reasons why he shouldn't take it.

"That's a brand-new car."

"I know it."

"You've only had your driver's license a few weeks."

"I know it."

"Youth camp is four hundred miles away."

"I know it."

"What makes you think you can have the car?" I finally asked.

"Well, I want to go to youth camp," Paul responded simply.

"You're not taking that new car four hundred miles to youth camp," I said.

"Oh, I forgot. I need the credit card, too."

"I'm not going to give you the car," I countered.

"I've been driving for a year with a permit," he reasoned, correctly.

"Just don't even ask me," I retorted. "I said no and that's it. I don't want to hear it again."

Case closed.

Paul turned and kicked at the floor, flushed with anger and disappointment. He walked down the hall to his room and grasped the doorknob to push the door open. Only he did not turn the knob quite far enough, and the door stood firm.

In that moment of frustration, Paul had had enough. Before he could think twice, he had given the door a violent kick.

When he closed the door behind him, there was a gaping hole in it.

I was still standing in the kitchen where I had just uttered my decree. When I heard the crash, an immediate surge of fury welled up inside me.

I'll teach him.

But the Holy Spirit stepped in, silently, unobtrusively, yet urgently, and whispered a word to my heart: *"Fathers, do not provoke your children to wrath"* (Ephesians 6:4).

In only a split second, my entire attitude completely changed. A grieving swept over me, and I felt the hot tears of remorse begin to sting my eyes. I walked into the garage, knelt before the Lord, and asked God for forgiveness for what I had done to my son.

Forty minutes later, I walked back out into the hall toward Paul's room. The Holy Spirit had humbled me.

I opened the damaged door, a somber symbol of my own dictatorial authoritarianism. Big words, but big sin. Paul was still sitting on the edge of his bed, elbows on knees, head in hands. Forty minutes after our angry exchange, there were still tears in his eyes.

I sat down beside him.

"Paul, I sinned against you," I said quietly. "I'm your dad, but I provoked you to wrath. I want you to know that I love you, and I ask you to forgive me."

I handed him the credit card and the keys.

"You go to camp."

He went. It was there that God took hold of his life. He was called to a ministry at that youth camp, and today he is one of the Christian world's foremost television producers.

The old saying goes, "It takes a man to admit he's wrong." That old saying is still around after so long a time because it's still right.

If you've never been willing to accept responsibility for your sins, and ask forgiveness, you can never know true manhood.

Forgiveness is a release.

When God forgives us, He releases us from that sin forever. He will never remember it against us again. What joy in knowing that!

Men need to know how to forgive the same way.

I was in Cleveland, and at the conclusion of the ministry, a man asked me to agree with him for the salvation of his two sons. As we started to pray, he said, "They are both alcoholics, and I know that if the Lord saves them they will be freed from that. Their families won't be hurt anymore."

I bowed my head to pray with him, then stopped and looked at him and asked him to look at me. He still had his head bowed.

There was some noise around us at the time, so I repeated myself in order to get his attention. His head snapped up.

"Were you ever an alcoholic?" I asked him. He hesitated to answer. He had been a believer for many years, and that was all in the past. He did not want to have that brought up to him again. Also, there were people standing nearby, and it was somewhat embarrassing to him.

But I pressed the point.

"Have you ever been an alcoholic?" I asked again.

"Yes," he answered softly.

"Were your children at home at the time?"

"Yes."

> **In forgiving someone's sins, we release them, but when we do not, those sins are retained.**

"Have you ever gone to your children and asked them to forgive you for being an alcoholic when they were young boys at home?"

"Oh, I'm sure they have," the man replied.

"That's not the issue," I retorted. "Have you ever gone to your sons and deliberately sat down with them and said to them, 'Forgive me for being an alcoholic and acting like I did when you were at home'?"

The man looked down, "No."

"Then I'll pray the prayer of agreement with you," I stated, "and I'll believe God with you for the salvation of your sons—under one condition."

"What's that?" he wondered.

"That you will go to your sons and ask them to forgive you of your alcoholism," I said, and then looked intently at him, waiting for his answer.

He returned my gaze, then agreed, and we prayed.

In forgiving someone's sins, we release them, but when we do not forgive them, those sins are retained. It is a kingdom principle.

That man's sons hated his alcoholism. They never forgave him for it. Because they never forgave him, they retained their father's sin and became like the thing they hated. Hate binds it to you. They bound themselves to their father's sin.

THERE'S A HOLE IN THE DOOR

Several years ago in Washington, D.C., a woman came up to me after a service at a Presbyterian church. There were tears in her eyes. Tears of gratitude, I was to discover.

"I just want to thank you," she said tearfully, "for what you said tonight."

She began to tell her story. Her husband was in the upper echelons of Jimmy Carter's administration, held in high esteem among all his peers. They were both educated, refined, cultured, and sophisticated people.

"I've always had a good rapport with people, and a very healthy self-image," the woman told me. "But about a year ago, I began having problems with my two daughters. I couldn't understand it. I began to question myself as to my own abilities as a mother, and even as a wife."

She began searching for answers and had turned to prayer and God's Word. In her searching, she came to know Jesus Christ as her personal Savior, and her husband soon followed in faith.

"Two weeks ago," she recalled, "I suddenly realized I was making the same mistakes with my girls that my mother had made with me. And my girls were reacting the same way to me that I had reacted to my mother. I hated myself for it, but I did not know what to do about it until tonight."

The meeting that night had been a turning point for her.

"Tonight, for the first time in my life, I forgave my mother for what she did to me. I released it out of my life, but I know I could never have done it by myself. I needed the Holy Spirit.

"Now," she finished, "I can hardly wait to get home to my girls. I know I'm free from the past, and I will never repeat that mistake again."

It had to be forgiven in order to be released.

In fact, I was in a church not too long ago and realized that this principle can hold true for entire congregations.

Years before, there was some great opposition between the pastor and the congregation. He left amid much bitterness and hard feelings.

When I was there, the pastor they had at that time was another in a long succession of them. They had all come to that congregation with high hopes and godly desires for success. However, each, in turn, had difficulties with the congregation and left. That congregation was bound to repetitious failure by their lack of forgiveness of that first pastor.

When you do not forgive someone's sin against you, you bear that sin; you carry it. You also make the same mistake again and again, with person after person.

In Charlotte, North Carolina, there was a man who had never forgiven his first business partner for running off with all the money, leaving him to pay the debts. The angry man continued to have problems in business until the night that he forgave the original partner. Today, he is enjoying a success he never had before.

A space scientist in California heard me teach this principle of forgiveness, and it changed his life. He and his father had not spoken during the last fifteen years of his father's life. His father had died twenty years before. That meant thirty-five years of unforgiveness.

The problem now was that the scientist and his daughter had not spoken in two years. She had even moved to Hawaii to get away from him. That night he realized that he was making the same mistake with his daughter, and he was suffering the same consequences as his father had with him. His father had been dead all these years; what should he do?

It was still essential that he forgive his dad, even after all those years. We prayed together and he received the release that he needed. That night, after the meeting, he wrote his daughter a lengthy letter, asking forgiveness and telling her things she had never known before. I saw him some weeks later; they had been reconciled, and he was making plans to fly to Hawaii to see her and his grandchildren.

Many fathers believe it is weak to admit when they have failed their children, or sinned against them, and to ask their forgiveness. Nothing could be further from the truth.

It is part of your maximized manhood. It is Christlike to give and receive forgiveness.

It is a documented fact that most parents who abuse their children were themselves abused children. What so many social workers, school counselors, and police detectives do not understand is the principle that Jesus taught. It is basic to human life.

Unforgiven sins pass from father to son, mother to daughter, generation to generation.

Sins are not hereditary.

They are unforgiven, and, in their retention, passed from father to son, mother to daughter, generation to generation. Every great revival in the history of the world has provided the release necessary for that generation. This generation needs release: you need release.

Do you hold unforgiveness toward your own parents, business partners, or friends?

Do you see your mistakes being relived in your children?

It is a cycle that can be broken by only one thing: forgiveness.

The late Harry Chapin, a master songwriter and storyteller, left us the haunting lyrics of "Cat's in the Cradle." It's a cycle we need to break in our lives today.

A child arrived just the other day,
He came to the world in the usual way.
But there were planes to catch, and bills to pay.
He learned to walk while I was away.
And he was talking 'fore I knew it,
And as he grew, He'd say,
"I'm gonna be like you, Dad.
You know I'm gonna be like you."

And the cat's in the cradle and the silver spoon,
Little boy blue and the man in the moon.
"When you coming home, Dad?"

"I don't know when,
But we'll get together then.
You know we'll have a good time then."
I've long since retired, and my son's moved away.
I called him up just the other day.
I said, "I'd like to see you if you don't mind."
He said, "I'd love to, Dad, if I could find the time.
You see, my new job's a hassle,
And the kid's got the flu,
But it's sure nice talking to you, Dad,
It's been sure nice talking to you."
And as I hung up the phone, it occurred to me,
He'd grown up just like me.
My boy was just like me.[*]

---

[*] Excerpt from song titled "Cat's in the Cradle" by Harry Chapin and Randy Chapin. © Story Songs, LTD, 1974. Used by permission. All rights reserved.

CHAPTER 6

TENDER AND TOUGH

*T*he 700 Club invited me to appear as a guest, and I was happy to accept the invitation. Several years before, I had been in a staff position as the "minister at large," and this was like an old home week, going back to meet and greet everyone.

Both Pat Robertson and Ben Kinchlow, the usual hosts, were gone that week, and in their place was a precious Christian couple. Once deeply involved in the world, they were now converted, and their love for the Lord Jesus Christ caused them to commit their entire lives to Him. This brought a completely new lifestyle to both of them. They are tireless, effervescent workers for the cause of Christ.

I have great admiration for both of them.

But we argued that day, in a friendly, yet serious, way.

And—before a live audience on a live program with millions watching.

The 700 Club's executive producer invited me to appear so that I could talk about ministering to men.

During the interview, I mentioned the principle that *balance is the key to life*.

"Because balance is the key to life," I said, "men must learn to be both tender *and* tough."

The female cohost blinked hard, and her eyebrows drew together sharply. She reacted immediately to the word *tough*, and she said so.

"My husband would never be tough with me," she insisted. "And if he were, I wouldn't like it."

"Nevertheless," I countered—as diplomatically as I knew how—"the man must be the leader in the home, and sometimes that requires toughness. Not roughness, but toughness."

> **Leadership in the home by the man requires toughness as well as tenderness.**

"There needs to be equality in the home between the man and the woman," she insisted.

"I never denied that," I responded. "But the man must lead, and—"

She jumped in again. She may have been her husband's equal at home, but on that program, at that moment, she was the leader. However, the point still stands: leadership in the home by the man requires toughness as well as tenderness.

The balance must be kept.

With children, the reward must balance the punishment, the caress must balance the spanking, the commendation must balance the correction.

Perhaps years ago, as a general rule, parents, educators, and political leaders may have erred on the side of toughness, but today it is the softness that is killing us. We must learn to be ruthless with ourselves at times.

Affections, desires, appetites—all must be dealt with in discipline. Even love must be disciplined, or we will love what will kill us.

Discipline requires toughness.

My wife and I had a friend years ago who lost her husband through death. He had been dear to her; they loved each other. After his death, she defied emotional healing, refusing to give up her attachment to him. She kept everything in the house just the way it was the last day he was home. Nothing changed. She continued to talk about him in the present tense. She loved him tenderly.

Tenderness destroyed her.

She failed to discipline her emotions and her thought-life, and in so doing, she refused to admit to herself that he had died. She created no new life for herself, nor did she allow God to work in her behalf and create one for her.

Even love must be disciplined, or we will love what will kill us.

Where once she had friends, a loving husband, and a full life, she was soon left with only her memories and a closetful of clothes. It was a self-created loneliness and isolation.

Ultimately, the tenderness made it tough on her.

Jesus was a perfect balance of the tender and tough.

He revealed His tenderness in His messages of love, His actions of healing and comforting, His death on the cross.

But the same Jesus who swept little children up into His arms gripped that scourge of cords and drove the money changers out of the temple. Some "sissified" paintings of Jesus come nowhere near showing the real character of Him who was both Son of Man and Son of God.

Jesus was a fearless leader, defeating Satan, casting out demons, commanding nature, rebuking hypocrites.

He had a nobility of character and a full complement of virtues that can be reproduced in us today—by the same Holy Spirit who dwelt in Him.

God wants to reproduce this manhood in all men.

What kind of manhood?

Christlikeness!

Christlikeness and manhood are synonymous.

So are Christlikeness and womanhood.

When the life of Jesus comes forth in both men or women, they are maximized. The fullness of their personality and character are brought forth.

The highest good of every individual is to be like Jesus. God has made everything conform to that ultimate purpose: to produce Christlikeness in us, to make us into His own image.

Since to be like Jesus—Christlike—requires a certain ruthlessness, manhood does also.

The concept of true manhood was brought home to me by Dr. C. E. Britton, a "Prince of the Pulpit." He was the victim of a childhood spinal injury and stood less than five feet tall. Yet in spite of his physical stature, Dr. Britton was a man's man, pastoring Bethany Church in Alhambra, California, for more than forty years. He was one of the finest men I have ever known. He never experienced a night without pain, yet he faithfully and marvelously discipled tremendous men of God and watched them establish great worldwide ministries.

Christlikeness and manhood are synonymous.

Dr. Britton was ministering one Sunday morning from Luke 13. He pointed out that just as the farmer expects figs under the leaves of his fig trees, so God expects fruit from our lives. The result, the product of the inner working of God in our lives, will be visible fruit. And since we belong to Him, God has a right to expect fruit.

That fruit is "Manhood."

Whatever God plants, He wants it to produce.

Orange trees produce oranges. Grapevines produce grapes. Fig trees produce figs. You do not get lemons from grapevines, nor figs from an orange tree.

Men, God created us as men and planted His Spirit within us; He expects to reap the fruit of manhood.

What happens if we refuse to allow this fruit to be produced in us?

In Luke 13, Jesus told His disciples that if the tree did not produce fruit after a certain time, then cut it down.

In John 15:2, Jesus essentially said, "If it doesn't produce, lop it off." That same principle applies to you and me. God has put all the nutrients of His grace, love, and truth into this world through Jesus Christ. To reject His salvation is to be lopped off eternally. Produce—be fruitful—or be cut off. This principle of reproduction holds true in every area of life.

> **Whatever God plants, He wants it to produce.**

A businessman was failing in his business. My friend was retained to examine and analyze the problem, then make the recommendations that would cause a turnabout. I'm sure the businessman wasn't prepared for the findings.

His problems were his relatives. He had hired many of them to work for him, but they weren't producing. Financially, his relatives were killing him. But because of the intricacy of the relationships, he could not discipline or fire them; so the business was lost. He might still have that business today if he had said, "Produce, or be lopped off."

His tenderness and toughness were out of balance.

Churches can be that way. Even though someone has not been productive for years, he or she is left in a position through sentiment. A church I know of was in constant turmoil during their worship services. The pastor was frustrated to tears by the deadness of the singing, the dirge-like quality dragging through the hymns. But it seemed to him there was nothing he could do because the organist who was causing the problem had been there for twenty years, and no one wanted to remove her from her place. Besides, she was related to many in the congregation.

What the pastor needed to do was tell her and the entire group of relations, in love, "Produce, or get lopped off."

"Repentance from dead works" is not only the forsaking of the works of the flesh to abide in Christ. It is also a principle of the kingdom that has broader meaning and scope. Whatever you are doing that is not productive in life is a dead work. It needs to be repented of—forsaken. Do something productive instead.

> **The kingdom of God is based on truth, not human sentiment.**

Don't retain it through sentiment if it's a dead work.

Think of all the unnecessary burdens people carry in their lives because of sentiment, and the truth is they despise them and want to quit them, but they don't because of sentimentality.

The kingdom of God is based on truth, not human sentiment.

Decisions must be made the same way.

Decision-making is one of the marks of a man.

Every successful man I know is decisive.

TENDER AND TOUGH

While ministering with the Christian Broadcasting Network years ago, I often found myself counseling, visiting, or just being friendly with the personnel. It was not uncommon to go from the stock room to the presidential suite. Only then it was not much of a suite—more like a working closet. During those days, I saw much of the decision-making process firsthand.

CBN, at that time, was involved in presenting good music, and also in publishing it. There was an in-house entity called *Housetop Records.* The philosophy in having it was that it would not only produce musicians and music, but money as well. The profits would help to subsidize *The 700 Club.* Only there were no profits.

A cost analyst was assigned to do an in-depth study and analysis of *Housetop's* success. After studying the records, analyzing the financial situation, projecting its future, and condensing it into a succinct, but comprehensive, report, the cost analyst submitted it all to Pat Robertson.

Pat studied it carefully, saw the deficit, realized the drain on CBN finances, prayed, and made a decision. The deficit was heavy, and the prospects of profits were remote. Having made his decision, Pat prayed again. It was obvious what needed to be done, but he wanted to make sure that he did it right.

He took it home with him for the weekend.

Monday morning, without hesitation, Pat Robertson simply dictated a memo that said: "As of this date, there is no more *Housetop Records."*

An awkward period of dismissals and reshuffling of personnel always follows such a decision. But it had to be done for the good of the ministry. By letting it continue, the entire ministry could have been hurt.

Jesus said, "If it doesn't produce, lop it off."

It took a certain ruthless courage to make that decision, and yet by sentimentalizing over the options, Pat could have squandered countless donor dollars and immeasurable resources for God's kingdom.

Decisions. Toughness. Leadership.

The marks of a man.

There are times when every man must be tough.

My children know that I can make decisions, have made them, and stand by them. But there are times in everyday life when it can become amusing.

We were in St. Louis years ago for one of the largest Christian gatherings in the Midwest. I was coordinating the event, and all I had to do to make it successful was have two hundred churches all do the same thing at the same time. That's all? It took six months.

My family joined me during the week, together with hundreds of cooperating workers and thousands of people. Everyone was enjoying it all, except me. I had to coordinate every activity, oversee each detail, and make it all seem as smooth as glass.

In addition to all that, my wife and I, and our two daughters, all had to stay in one hotel suite. Tension ran high in me. One morning in the middle of the week, the girls argued about where to go and what to do. I had had my fill of it.

I turned to them and said emphatically, "Lois, you will go to the Arch monument, and Jo, you will stay with your mother. I am going to work, and I don't want to hear another word!"

They had all learned to recognize that tone of voice, so no one said anything as I prepared to leave the room. As I turned the door knob, I remembered that I had not had my devotions. Hurriedly I went back, picked up the Bible, glanced at a few verses, then knelt at the foot of the bed to say "Good morning" to the

Lord. After a few moments kneeling there, I sensed someone standing nearby, and I knew it was not Him.

I slowly raised my head, and looked at my wife standing there with brush in hand. She was looking down at me benevolently as I knelt there at the foot of the bed.

She queried, oh, so softly, "Are you asking or telling?"

As she turned and walked quietly away, I dissolved into laughter along with my daughters, and the tension was gone.

Women desire their men to make decisions. Not as a dictator, but as a leader. There is a vast difference. Dictators make decisions based on personal preference, or selfish gratification, but leaders make decisions based on what is best for their followers.

> **Women desire their men to make decisions. Not as a dictator, but as a leader.**

Nations, families, women, children—all need decision makers. Decisions are not always right, but they are always decisions. Even no decision is a decision by default.

Years ago I heard a friend say that a man who straddles the fence will get hurt badly when he falls. It's dangerous.

Indecisiveness creates instability. Scripture states that the *"double minded man is unstable in all his ways"* (James 1:8 KJV).

Second-guessing reflects a lack of confidence in a decision already made. If a decision is made and it proves to have been faulty or wrong, admit it, repent of it, learn from it, and go on from that point.

If God forgives us, but we do not forgive ourselves, we make ourselves greater than Him. Wisely forgetting the past is part of man's maturing. It is essential to real manhood. It is unfair to demand forgiveness for the same sin over and over again. Once forgiven, it is to be wisely forgotten. Wisely forgetting is not putting it out of our minds; it is never again holding that sin against anyone.

Crying over spilled milk, living with regret, or carrying past mistakes are all wrong. Living with past mistakes is a mistake in itself.

Owen Carr, the founder of Chicago's Christian television station, relates in his book, *The Battle Is the Lord's,* how his skeptical father reacted to the news that Owen was going into the ministry.

> **If God forgives us, but we do not forgive ourselves, we make ourselves greater than Him.**

"If you're going to start, don't stop!" his dad told young Owen. "And if you're going to stop, don't start!"

Men have the ultimate responsibility for their decisions.

The essence of maturity is the acceptance of that responsibility. And maturity is the essence of manhood.

The popular notion is that maturity comes with age. Not true. You get old with age. Maturing comes by the acceptance of responsibility—in every area of life.

Accepting responsibility for our failures is the substance on which success rests. No one can be responsible for success unless he is willing to accept responsibility for failure as well. This is true in business, marriage, and all of life.

No one should ever be surprised by the latest statistics on runaway children. They are sad, but they should not shock us. Runaway children are only mimicking what they have learned from their runaway parents—most often their fathers. In the state of California, when I was serving on the Committee for Children and Youth, four hundred thousand women lived alone with their children because their husbands ran away from home.

Those four hundred thousand California men could not, would not, or did not choose to accept the responsibility of being a husband and father, at least not according to most marriage vows.

Divorce used to be a bad word. Today, it is fashionable. Still, it is usually just a cover-up for the evasion of responsibility.

Many men flit from woman to woman, place to place, acting out their version of the popular "macho" man. The ability to procreate is not necessarily the evidence of manhood. In truth, they are childlike men, immature in spirit, infantile in understanding, living on the thin surface of life, rootless, without depth, without character.

The essence of maturity is the acceptance of responsibility.

Some men are mature at seventeen. Others are immature at seventy.

Churches are afflicted with immature males—men who have shamefully forfeited spiritual leadership, abandoning it to the women. Having successfully turned over the reins of discipline in the home, the man now moves to slough off his responsibility in the church. In parish after parish, women exercise the gifts of the Spirit; women teach, organize, lead, and funnel the praises and worship to the Father.

It is possible to get spirituality from women, but strength always comes from men. A church, a family, a nation is only as strong as its men.

Men, you are accountable.

There is no sleek escape chute.

God requires manhood from all men.

When a man is born again and forgiven of his sins, the slate is wiped clean; the heart has been cleansed. But the commandments of God need to be written on that fresh, blank slate. That new Christian must read the Word of God and commune with the Father through prayer. He must begin to live in the Spirit. The new heart is like Moses' stone tablets on which God wrote. The Holy Spirit inscribes God's Word on our hearts as we study and meditate on the Word.

The man who has been a believer for many years and has never gone beyond memorizing John 3:16 is just as immature as the man who received Christ yesterday!

His salvation makes very little difference. He is far from Canaan Land. He has never begun to maximize his potential as a man in Christ Jesus.

The more Word you have in you, the more Word-like, Christlike, you become.

His spiritual immaturity is likely to lead him into sin, immorality, unethical conduct, and a whole wide range of temptations. He has never rooted himself in the Word. Never learned the Scriptures that make us wise and help us determine the course of our conduct, the mode of our speech, the attitudes of our heart, and the foundation for our conscience.

The more Word you have in you, the more Word-like, the more Christlike, you become. The Word must be acquired in spirit.

The less Word, the less Word-like, the less Christlike, you become. It's an elementary formula, but it separates the men from the boys.

Manhood and Christlikeness are synonymous.

You'll hear me say that over and over again because it's true. Only the greatness of Christ in our lives can make us great. Nothing else. It's the reason John the Baptist said, *"He must increase, but I must decrease"* (John 3:30). It's the reason we must allow God to produce the fruit of manhood in our lives.

The parable of the Prodigal Son is the story of humanity. When the Prodigal *"came to himself"* (Luke 15:17) and returned to his father's house, he was forgiven, cleansed, and restored to his rightful position.

When he accepted the responsibility for his own actions, repented of them, and asked for forgiveness, his whole life changed.

Yours can, too. You can enter into a whole new Canaan Land.

But the only way is to develop true "manhood."

Christlikeness.

CHAPTER 7

IS THERE A PRIEST IN THE HOUSE?

There's a priest in every house. God has designated the man to play the part. Bible student or not, men, you're the priest.

Whether you believe it, receive it, live it, or ignore it, you're the priest. It's the job of the priest to minister not only to the Lord, but also to the ones entrusted to his care. This does not mean that a family cannot reach God except through the man. It means a man must minister to his wife and children.

Such a ministry has to be worked at. It takes a real man to accomplish it successfully. But God gives all the directions we need in His Guidebook.

Most men fail to recognize that they have to fulfill a ministry as priest in their homes.

One day the phone rang in my office. When I answered, my female caller wanted to know if I was the Dr. Cole who had seminars for men. When she was assured that I was the one she wanted, she asked for a few minutes of my time. Her voice was tinged with anxiety; there was a tear in it.

"I'm calling you with fear and trembling," she began, "because I don't want my husband to know that I'm talking to you.

"I know you talk to men. I have listened to your tapes, and I think they are powerful in speaking to men.

"I want you to tell men how we women really feel."

She had my attention with that.

"I could never talk to my pastor or anyone here in my town and tell them what I'm telling you," she went on. "They would never understand.

"My husband is a good man. He never misses a church service. He's hardly ever late. We both work in the church. I teach Sunday school, while he is an usher. We are both Christians and love the Lord."

I waited for her to get to the point. She did. "But in all the years we have been married," the woman said, her voice draped in sadness, "my husband has never talked to me in our home about the things of God. We talk about everything else, but he just has never talked about the things of God. It was fifteen years after our wedding before he ever prayed in front of me, and then it was only because I was sick, and I asked him to."

I could hear her hurt.

"He takes care to do everything he can for me. I feel terrible talking about him behind his back, but I'm so lonely. I just don't know what else to do right now. *A part of my life is missing because he has never taken the lead in praying or talking about the Lord.*

"When my children were home, I had someone to read the Bible and pray with because I would do it with them. Now, they are all gone. The last one was married and left home less than a year ago. My husband makes enough money that I don't have to work, and so I'm home most of the time. It isn't just because the children are gone that I'm lonely. I just don't have any leadership from my husband.

"Please tell the men wherever you go that we women want them to be leaders in the home in every way—especially to lead us in prayer and the study of God's Word. If he would just change and be a leader, I could love him even more.

"Please understand. I love my husband. It's just that I get so hungry for him to take his place. I don't want to step in and take it. That isn't right. I know a lot of women do, but I don't think it's right.

"Thank you for listening to me and please, please, tell the men of America that we want them to be men."

The priest of the house must pray for his wife.

Prayer produces intimacy.

You become intimate with the One to whom you pray, the one for whom you pray, and the one with whom you pray.

> **You become intimate with the One to whom you pray, the one for whom you pray, and the one with whom you pray.**

Moses went up to Mount Sinai, the place of prayer, and stayed so long that finally God was able to speak to him as friend to friend. Why?

Because prayer produces intimacy.

Jesus had become so intimate with the Father in prayer that on the Mount of Transfiguration the glory of the Father's presence shone through Him.

On the Day of Pentecost, the disciples were endued with power because they were praying together. Their prayer produced such an intimacy that they were *"all with one accord"* (Acts 2:1), and their prayer of agreement brought power.

When a man prays with his wife, he becomes intimate with her. In true spiritual prayer, the intimacy developed is far greater than physical union. It is in spirit.

A woman praying for her husband develops an intimacy with him in spirit that draws her to him. She identifies with his needs and thus helps to meet them.

The failure of the man to pray for his wife means that he can have a physical intimacy, but he does not develop the intimacy of spirit that produces true oneness.

Sexual relations are one thing; spiritual union is another. If you really want to be one with your wife, then pray for her and with her.

> **If you really want to be one with your wife, then pray for her and with her.**

This is the reason for the motto, "The family that prays together stays together."

Every woman needs to be unique in her own eyes. A man ministering to his wife is to help establish this. But if he doesn't pray for her, her deepest needs receive no attention.

Every woman craves the intimacy of some man. She was made that way. When she is denied that intimacy with her husband, her nature is to seek out an alternative source. Men who know their wives in prayer also know them in the living room, kitchen, and bedroom.

If, as you read this, you have not prayed for your wife, stop—right now—and ask God to forgive you. Begin to change this very moment. Don't even read another word until you have prayed for her.

There, that's more like it.

I was ministering in Canada, speaking with real vehemence about the need for men to minister in prayer. The day after the meeting, a man came up to me, grinning somewhat sheepishly. His wife stood by his side, beaming as he told me, "Last night you kicked me in the teeth when I heard you talking about prayer. But I prayed with my wife for the first time in eleven years, and today we are closer than we ever were."

Ministry is not just preaching.

Ministry is prayer.

Perhaps here I should take a moment to speak to women. This is an important point.

Women may have an easier time praying for their husbands, but some women try to play God. They attempt to create their husbands in their own image of what he should be, not letting God create the man *"in His own image"* (Genesis 1:27).

This problem occurs even before marriage. Women seem to have a greater tendency to give their fiancés the benefit of the doubt when it comes to character flaws. I can't count the number of women who have met and married alcoholics, thinking they could change their husbands after the wedding by showering them with love.

The classic statement of error is: "I thought all he needed was the love of a good woman."

Whatever a man is when he is single, he is more of when he is married, unless Christ is there to make a difference.

The same thing happens with Christian women. They desire their unsaved husbands to share in the good news of Jesus Christ, and they desire it so much that they often err. They seem to believe that "no man comes to the Father except his *wife* draws him."

No woman draws a man to God; the Holy Spirit does that.

Innumerable women have run their bodies, minds, and souls to the point of frenzy, trying to supplant the work of God's Holy Spirit. Over and over counselors tell women, "Don't play God."

Sure, the man is to be the priest, but God has to lead him into it. It can't be a woman pushing him. A woman's push is helpful only when a man is already being pulled or led by God's Spirit into being what God wants him to be.

Men can change habits; only God can change a nature.

Women, don't play God!

The woman who finds herself with an unbelieving husband on her hands—or a Christian husband less than maximized in his potential manhood—has two key steps offered to her in the Scriptures.

> **Men can change habits; only God can change a nature.**

First, make sure you have forgiven your husband of all his sins. Many wives do not forgive their husbands. Without forgiveness, she holds his sins against him and binds them to him. Forgiveness opens; unforgiveness closes. Forgiveness releases; unforgiveness binds.

Many men who genuinely desire to become the man God wants them to be find themselves battling to be free from their wives' bondage of unforgiveness.

Second, love him. What a simple statement, and yet it is God's formula for marital success. *The Amplified Bible* says it this way: *"You married women, be submissive to your own husbands...and [adapt yourselves to them], so that even if they do not obey the Word [of God], they may be won over not by discussion but by the [godly] lives of their wives, when they observe the pure and modest way in which you conduct yourselves, together with your reverence [for your husband; you are to feel for him all that reverence includes: to respect, defer to, revere him—to honor, esteem, appreciate, prize, and in the human sense to adore him, that is, to admire, praise, be devoted to, deeply love and enjoy your husband]"* (1 Peter 3:1–2 AMP).

That is God's divine pattern to cause a man to desire to change and to enable him to minister to his wife. This was God's intention ever since Eve was first called Adam's "helpmate."

Still, men, the burden of proof is on you. God holds the man responsible for becoming the priest of the house. Learn to minister to your wife.

A man ministers to his wife by giving her assurance.

Every woman needs to know she is unique to her man.

That's why even women who are promiscuous feel a measure of guilt in having sexual relations without any love. So prior to submitting to a man's lovemaking, they ask the age-old question, "Do you love me?"

> **You assure your wife of your love when you tell her she is the one God wanted you to have.**

Mechanical sex cannot satisfy the desire for true intimacy.

You assure your wife of your love for her when you tell her she is the one God wanted you to have.

We are committed to what we confess.

The marriage vow is a confession that causes commitment, but a lack of commitment is a major issue facing couples today. Many men feel they were coerced into marriage, manipulated or cornered by circumstances. As a result, they wonder about the imagined destiny that might have been.

Likewise, when a woman marries because of pregnancy or financial insecurity or some other pressure, she is often uncertain that her husband is God-given.

Husbands and wives both, in the midst of such uncertainty, look at others and fantasize, "Was he the one?" "What would it have been like with her?"

All of this decomposes the body of marriage relationships.

Every husband needs to realize that the sacredness of the marriage union is God's highest priority in any marriage. Every man needs to settle it in his mind: "She's the one." Having done that, he must confess it to himself and to her. Such a confession is crucial.

Remember: we are committed to what we confess.

You minister to your wife when you confess that she is the one for you. It's her assurance. Her security.

Men are priests. They must minister.

But as you see, ministry is far beyond preaching.

Ministry is loving.

Today's perversion of morals has created philosophies that fragment marriages, homes, and society. Some men have the attitude that the doctrine of separation of church and state means that anything religious, sacred, or spiritual should be relegated to the church worship hour, and they can do as they please the rest of the time. Wrong.

Men are priests. They must minister.

A man never stops ministering.

It's his life.

He ministers when he sells a car, contracts a building, builds a computer, executes corporate decisions—everything in life is ministry. Many men, after ministering to people all day, are in no mood to minister at home in the evening.

The great complaint among wives—especially ministers' wives—is: "My husband can minister to the whole world, but he can't minister to me."

The man defends himself on the basis of busyness, fatigue, workload, economic pressure, client anxiety, and he is ministering to the whole world. Admittedly, it is taxing.

Upon arriving home, he wants to be ministered to, not have to minister. But the truth is that ministry in the home comes first.

Today's modern man trades wives and keeps businesses.

Even Christian husbands are subject to error without realizing it.

I have seen over and over again the same syndrome at work in countless lives: couples fall in love and marry, but as business grows, children come, church needs demand attention—more and more they do things with the kids, for the church, or for their businesses.

> **Men don't own anything; they are only stewards.**

What they need to realize is that they fell in love with each other, and after everything else is gone they will still have each other, provided they have been good stewards of their marriages.

God made man to be a leader and a steward.

Men don't own anything; they are only stewards.

Health, marriage, children, lands, businesses, their wives' love—over all these men are only stewards. Everything belongs to God; He gave it all to us. It is what we do with it, how we take care of it, for which we must give an account.

Men make the mistake, or sin, of thinking they are possessors. That thinking causes them to act independently of God. And that is where all our problems begin. Adam acted independently of God, and look at us now!

Men, you don't possess your wife's love. You are only a steward of it. It is God's gift to you.

Be a good steward. Be the priest. Minister.

Minister to your wife.

Leave your children for a few days with grandparents or friends. Take time from your job, and get away together—just the two of you. Fall in love all over again. Minister to her. That is the reason for her submission.

Every married couple needs to have a honeymoon at least every six months, for at least a long four-day weekend. Without that special time together, you may find, after a quarter of a century of marriage, with the children gone, that you have forgotten how to love or communicate, and you face separation.

Minister.

Pray for her and with her. Develop your intimacy.

Confess she is your wife. Minister assurance. That is loving her.

Take her away and give her your undivided attention.

Fall in love again periodically.

Men, you don't have any options.

It is God who called you to be the priest in your home.

Is there a priest in your home?

CHAPTER 8

THE ONE-DOLLAR TIP

While I was general manager of a television station, it fell my lot to fire a young man. Tom had all the ingredients of great success, but he was failing in his ministry.

As an executive with the station, he had the expertise to become financially successful, but he wasn't.

This was the fifth time he had tried to make a success of the ministry. He had pastored two different churches, each unhappily. He had moved to a business position in a ministry—and failed. Then he had taken a position as associate pastor in yet another church, but the results were always the same—unfruitful.

And now he had failed to produce at the television station. He knew it well. The dismissal came as no surprise.

"I don't know what to say to you, Tom," I told him as we talked that evening. "I don't know what to do for you. I want to help you, and the only thing that I can think of is that for some reason, some inexplicable reason, you are not believing God for answers to your prayers."

I was struggling to come up with the answers for him that would help him in the future, so that the string of failures could somehow be broken, and his pattern of life remade.

Tom acknowledged the truth of what I had said. He admitted to me that prayer had become very difficult for him. The only time he ever prayed any more, in fact, was in public, when called on in church services or Christian meetings.

He had not yet made the vital connection between this lack of prayer in his life and the struggle he always seemed to have on the job.

He was a third-generation Christian, the son and grandson of prominent, successful ministers. He had always tried to get by on the coattails of his heritage.

It had never worked.

But Tom was gracious. He knew I held no malice for him. He and his wife, Sue, invited my wife and me to dinner a few days later.

Then the puzzle began to come together.

Sue had set a perfectly lovely table. I commended her for it and commented that we were appreciative of the invitation to dinner.

"Yes, it sure is great to have you here for dinner tonight," Tom interjected playfully. "Now we'll get a good meal for a change."

Nancy and I glanced at each other, but maintained the casual conversation. A few minutes into the meal, Sue slipped out to the kitchen for a pitcher of juice. As she returned, I noticed how very proper and pleasant our hostess looked, carrying a sparkling pitcher and smiling warmly. But at the same moment, her husband quipped, "You know, my wife's from Arkansas; she only wore shoes because you're here."

Sue reddened, but said nothing.

Dinner proceeded, and the frequency of Tom's little barbs increased. Throughout the meal, and beyond, he kept giving those crooked little strokes to his wife, making her the butt of his humor.

Eventually, the nervous laughter fell into awkward conversation, but he did not let up. Tom thought he was being humorous. He was the only one who thought so.

As I sat in their house, I realized why Tom was not a success, why he had such trouble praying, and why he was not experiencing the blessings of God.

One paraphrased version of 1 Peter 3:7 says, "You husbands, treat your wives as joint heirs with you of the life of God, because if you don't, your prayers will not get ready answers."

Tom was ignoring Peter's stern advice to treat his wife as a "joint heir."

Because of that failing, Tom was not getting ready answers to his prayers. Since his prayer life was ineffective, he was failing in the ministry. Without ready answers to his prayers, his faith had grown weak, and without faith it is impossible to please God.

> **Your wife must be your joint heir—every bit as worthy as you think you are.**

Your wife must be your joint heir—every bit as worthy of consideration, appreciation, and affection as you think you are.

Moral support is not her job alone. Nor are the decisions of the home yours alone. No man in marriage can live or act independently of his wife.

Many men blame the boss because they don't get the promotion, or they blame the guy in the next office who snatched that job away, when the real reason can be found in their own lives. They are failing, stumbling, struggling, and falling short because they are not treating their wives as joint heirs.

Tom is not alone in his sin. The syndrome is epidemic. A man's demeaning his wife is one of the classic social practices of our age.

I thought of Sue's background. It was far different from Tom's, and the butt of his frequent jokes.

Her mother, a promiscuous woman, had dragged Sue through a dozen different public schools during her childhood and teen years. Sue's loneliness dogged her. A bright child, she engaged in every self-help program she could find to try to better herself, even at that tender age.

Finally, she was invited to attend a meeting with a youth group from a local church, and there she gave her heart to Christ. In her senior year in high school, she won a contest. The prize: a year's scholarship at a Bible college.

It was there she met Tom. As a third-generation ministerial student, he was steeped in the traditions of Christianity. He had been raised in church, a preacher's kid, and was "church wise." He knew everything that needed to be done, and how it needed to be done. Fondness between them was followed by love, love by marriage.

Tom and Sue launched themselves into ministry after Tom's graduation. She had no experience with the lifestyle, no background in this type of work. She really did not understand the demands and expectations of a preacher's wife. Tom did not take the time to teach her or explain much of it to her. Because he knew, he simply assumed she would know and act accordingly.

Assumption is life's *lowest level* of knowledge. Tom operated on a level of assumption with Sue.

THE ONE-DOLLAR TIP

In her state of ignorance, and fearing to ask, she made the inevitable mistakes of someone new to the parsonage. Sometimes—most times—they were embarrassing to her husband.

Tom reacted.

To cover his embarrassment, instead of patiently spending time explaining matters to her, he began to put her down, to make fun of her, to demean her in front of others.

Self-justification's process is to make yourself look right in your own eyes by placing your blame on someone else.

God's response had already been stated in 1 Peter. Tom stopped getting ready answers to his prayers.

The blessings of God stopped flowing in Tom's life and ministry.

Frustrated, and with his faith weakened, Tom became debilitated in prayer and eventually that realm of his life withered and virtually died. He could no longer believe God for the goals he wanted to accomplish in life, and success plunged into failure.

Tom, as per the pattern of men, justified himself in his own eyes by placing the blame on Sue. Of course, he never said so outright. He just began to make her the scapegoat by making her the object of ridicule.

Unable to accept responsibility for his own failures, he looked for, and found, the handiest scapegoat, and the process of demeaning her continued over the years.

What he needed to do—and what you need to do if you are like Tom—was to take Sue someplace all alone and open his heart to her. He needed to let that relationship be healed. He needed to change; then Sue could.

Of course, some men fail to treat their wives as joint heirs, yet they still succeed in business. But in almost every case, there can be found some other area of failing, some other breakdown in their lives that indicates this shortcoming.

If Dad treats Mom like chattel instead of a joint heir, the children observe it and reflect the same attitude in their actions.

Wives must be treated as joint heirs.

Murmuring against your wife, maligning her and demeaning her, will sap you of your manhood and keep you from having a maximized marriage.

Everything in this life appreciates or depreciates.

When it appreciates it gains value.

When it depreciates it loses value.

Human beings appreciate or depreciate, according to the value placed upon them.

Homes, cars, land, stocks—all appreciate or depreciate. They do so according to the value placed upon them.

Human beings also appreciate or depreciate, according to the value placed upon them.

When you appreciate a woman, she gains value—in her own eyes and in yours. When you depreciate her, she loses value—both in her eyes and in yours.

Tom had depreciated his wife, and in her loss of value in her own eyes as well as his, she had begun to be ineffective and feel inferior.

I can remember my own crisis point in this area.

Years ago, Nancy and I were pastoring a struggling new church in northern California. In fact, everything about me was struggling—me most of all.

I didn't understand what was happening.

I didn't know what to do about it.

We were remodeling the building in which we were worshipping, trying to make it as pleasant as possible.

A new, maple, hardwood floor was being laid, and in each spare moment I was working on it to speed the process.

Alone one afternoon, I was pounding nails into that floor.

With each blow of the hammer, I pounded out my own personal frustrations—frustrations toward God; frustrations toward my wife, Nancy; frustrations toward the struggling congregation; toward myself. I told God exactly how I felt.

"God, you've got to do something! God, you've got to change this situation! You've got to help me. Change these circumstances! Change Nancy! Change the congregation! You've got to help me!

"God, I need help!"

Nancy and I were living in a house with only four hundred and twenty square feet. We were agonizing over every penny, getting more and more on each other's frazzled nerves.

God heard my prayer.

God answered me.

Personally.

As I stood there, bent over from the waist, pounding nails, God opened my mind. He pressed the "Rewind" button on my mental tape recorder, and then He began to replay for me excerpts of my own words.

He reminded me of everything I had been saying about Nancy—each judgmental attitude toward her, every demeaning verbal stroke I had given her, each time I had depreciated her by some comment.

I loved my wife. Dearly.

Yet I had fallen into that same attitude common to man.

Nancy, because of her convenience, had become the target of my frustration, the object of my humor, and the scapegoat for my failures. It was not always by a direct method—just that constant murmuring.

I was stunned and shattered by the revelation. I felt the hot hand of shame against the back of my neck.

Then God did something for which I will ever be grateful.

He showed me her graciousness, virtues, loveliness, and beauty of spirit. I saw her as God saw her.

> **God showed me my wife's virtues. I saw her as God saw her.**

Instantly, I dropped the hammer and fell on that hard floor and asked God to forgive me. Deep within my spirit, I cried out to God, but this time altogether differently.

Then, still with that heavy apron of nails around my waist, I raised my hands toward heaven—unashamedly, without any reservation or hesitation—and lifted my voice openly.

"God forgive me for my attitude! Forgive me for the way I've regarded my wife! I want to love her! I want to appreciate her—not depreciate her. I receive her as your gift to me! I confess she is my wife! I thank you for her!"

My new spiritual floor was being laid.

Much later, broken and remodeled, I stood up, took off the apron of nails, and headed home. I walked next door to our tiny house, changed clothes, cleaned up, and went downtown. There I picked up a little gift and a simple Hallmark card.

It was dinnertime.

I walked into the kitchen where Nancy was and handed her the card and gift, giving her a kiss on the cheek.

"What's this for?" she asked, startled.

THE ONE-DOLLAR TIP

"Just because I love you," I told her honestly.

She looked at me a moment, perhaps checking her intuition to make sure of my proper motivation. You know how women are.

"Really?" she offered tentatively.

"Yes."

She opened the gift. Something simple, but she was thoroughly enthralled with it. She glowed over it, her eyes dancing.

We had soup for dinner. I wanted to appreciate her, not depreciate her.

"This," I declared with a flourish as we began to eat, "is the best soup you've ever made. And—it's hot."

Nancy looked at me somewhat blankly.

"What do you mean by that?"

I shrugged. "I just like my soup hot. I don't like it heated over a candle; I like it hot."

Nancy tilted her head a little to one side. "I didn't know that."

"I probably didn't tell you," I replied. "But it's really great soup. I really enjoy it, and I appreciate it."

Nancy took a moment to absorb the compliment, then she said, "Thank you."

So simple. Yet life changed that day.

Appreciation had begun its work. Depreciation's work was over. Finished.

It was a lasting change. Over twenty-seven years have passed since that day, and I have never forgotten that bowl of soup—nor the change God made in my life.

Our relationship has never been the same since.

Nancy's value began to multiply—in my eyes and in her own eyes. The quality of our home began to increase miraculously. The ministry took a new leap forward. Everything was different.

That's the day I began to refer to her as: *"The loveliest lady in the land."*

And she is.

She should have been born to royalty. She's gracious, charming, wise, beautiful, strong, and simply wonderful.

The more I appreciate her, the lovelier she becomes.

At the end of the meal, when Nancy had slipped away from the table and I was ready to leave to do some work, I took a dollar bill out of my pocket and put it under my plate. A dollar was not easy for us to come by in those early days. My gesture was not one of condescension, but of appreciation.

Not just saying it, but showing it.

I was already in the other room when she found it as she cleared the table. She held it in her hand as she walked in to me from the kitchen.

"What's this for?" she asked quizzically.

"Honey, when I go to a restaurant," I replied, "if I appreciate the meal and the service, I leave a little token of appreciation. Because the meal was so good tonight, I thought I'd leave a little token of appreciation. That's all. I just wanted you to know I love you and appreciate you."

She understood.

The tip of a lifetime.

CHAPTER 9

CHANGING HEADS

The silly old joke goes like this: In the back room of a funeral parlor, a widow came to view her late husband's body before the funeral was to begin. She was shocked to discover, however, that the mortician had put someone else's suit on her husband's body.

Looking around, she realized that the man in the next casket was in fact wearing her husband's suit.

More grief-stricken than ever, she called the mortician over to the casket and tearfully pointed out the problem. He promptly acted to correct the situation.

"Harry!" he shouted to one of his assistants. "Switch the heads on two and three!"

Horrible, but you'll never forget it.

And it illustrates something else that I don't want you ever to forget.

Change always comes from the top.

If it doesn't, it will come from revolution at the bottom.

A friend of mine named Al was a professional troubleshooter for failing businesses. His clients were companies on the verge of bankruptcy, dissolution, or other disasters.

Al was never called, in fact, until a company was in severe crisis. He enjoyed the work because, by the time he was called, the corporate officers were usually ready to listen to straight talk and swallow the bitter pill of truth. Survival always depended on change.

There was almost always a pattern to these corporate nightmares. You can have the greatest program but with poor personnel, fail; or you can have a poor program, with good personnel, and succeed. Personnel is always the problem, and personnel is always the solution. And the solution always originates through the man at the top.

"No company that is sick," Al told me one day, "can be healed and made financially healthy unless the man at the head is willing to change."

Al found that, almost without exception, the problems were caused by the chief executive officer.

"Unless he is willing to change," Al said, "there is no hope."

His method in dealing with companies became rather standard over a period of time. He would investigate their operating procedures, search their financial records, interview the personnel, and seek to know the problem from every conceivable perspective. During the course of it all, he made sure that he spent hours in the office of the head of the company.

In presenting his analysis, giving his evaluation, and making his recommendations in his report, he invariably included a change that needed to be made by the man at the top. This change involved his methods, motives, attitudes, relationships, or, at times, even his lifestyle.

That principle is applicable to every area of human life, including the family.

CHANGING HEADS

The man needs to change so that his family can change. The man needs to grow so that his family can grow. He sets the example.

Change is not change until it is change.

Most people judge others by their *actions,* and themselves by their *intentions.*

Intention to change is not change. Talking about changing, pledging it, making resolutions concerning it—none of these are change. None of these things will heal a hurting home.

The head of the house must change.

America has spent untold millions of dollars on efforts to prevent juvenile delinquency. For those youth who have become emotionally warped, criminally inclined, addicted, or just wayward, we have invested more millions in rehabilitation programs. For women, we have innumerable books, an over-abundance of seminars, and other helps to teach them to be good wives.

> **Intention to change is not change.**

Having done all that, we send our wives and children back to homes where the men have not changed, where they are still untaught. These men have, more often than not, created the problems of the wives and the children in the first place. Thus, the women and children are right back where they started.

Rehabilitated children and reformed wives will find frustration when they come home to unchanged fathers and husbands. Because the man is the head of the house, change is to start with him!

I live in Newport Beach, California, near a marvelous beach. The beach snuggles up to jetties on both sides of the isthmus that allows the boats to go in and out of Balboa Bay.

This beach has been my private closet for prayer, my meditation room, counseling chamber, and place of soul therapy. The jetty is the place of many watershed experiences both in my life and in the lives of others who have spent time with me there.

When Rick drove down from Oregon and called me, I told him to meet me at the jetty. He was deeply troubled.

There among the rocks, he told me that moving to Oregon had been a big mistake. He had gone there just to get away from everything—only to realize when he arrived that "everything" had come with him. He hadn't left anything at all. A strange consternation was boiling within him. He needed a change. He didn't have it, but he wanted it.

Just a few weeks before, he had been working on a house he was building. While out in the yard, he heard this inner voice say, "Let go." On other occasions, this same voice had said the same words. Though he had talked to others about it, he did not know what was happening. Then, while wondering about it all, he felt impressed to fly back to California, rent a car, and drive up to see me. He wanted to know what I thought was happening to him.

"Is it the Holy Spirit speaking to me," he wanted to know, "or the Devil or who?"

The more we talked, the more I realized God was at work in Rick's life. But Rick had yet to realize it.

"Honestly, I don't know what to do," he said helplessly. "I'm not happy with myself, my wife is not happy with me, and my children are unhappy. If something doesn't happen soon, I don't know what I'll do! And then, I keep hearing this voice inside me saying, 'Let go.'"

Rick had confessed Jesus Christ as his Savior several years before, but he had never made a total commitment. Some areas of his life were still very much under his own control instead of God's. As we talked and prayed together, the light began to dawn in Rick's heart.

It became crystal clear that it really was God speaking by His Spirit to Rick's heart. "Let go" meant to release himself totally into God's hands, trusting entirely in Him. Rick came to the realization that God was simply saying, "Let go of all your own ways, and depend on Me in the totality of life."

With that understanding, we prayed, agreeing with God. Rick, forsaking his old ways, submitted to the lordship of Jesus Christ in his life. In that moment, Rick became more of a man than he had ever been before.

> **God says, "Let go, and depend on Me in the totality of life."**

It is God working in us, *"both to will and to do for His good pleasure"* (Philippians 2:13), that brings forth true manhood in its various dimensions.

A change had taken place.

What would happen within his family?

Months later, Rick and Joan were sitting in my living room with several others. We were talking about our God-given goal of ministering to thousands of men throughout the nation.

Suddenly, I noticed that Joan was weeping. I asked her why.

"I'm not crying for me," she said, crying nonetheless. "I'm really crying for the other women who are going to have the same thing happen to them that happened to me. After Rick experienced that change in his life, he came home, and immediately things were different."

Then Joan explained the amazing results.

"We did not tell the kids what Rick had experienced. We just wanted to let everything happen naturally.

But three days after Rick returned home, my daughter came to me and said, 'Mommy, *what happened to Daddy? He's changed.*'"

Rick, Joan, and their children discovered that change comes from the head of the family.

"Whenever a man changes and becomes the man God wants him to be," Joan said emphatically, "it will bring a change to the woman and the children. I'm crying with happiness because I know what is going to happen to all those women who are like I was. The whole home changes when the man changes."

There was nothing magic about the jetty or the beach. But there was something new in Rick's heart and life. That's where the change was. He had a new attitude, a new approach to life, a new obedience to God. Now he was beginning to operate in the realm of divine wisdom rather than human wisdom.

> **When a man becomes who God wants him to be, it will bring change to the woman and children.**

He had taken responsibility for failure, exchanged it in prayer by repentance and faith, and become responsible for Christlike manhood. God's transcendent glory was at work in his life. Obedience to God's Word did it.

A ton of prayer will never produce what an ounce of obedience will. After all the praying, if you don't obey, you nullify the praying. Belief plus action equals faith.

Manhood isn't talked, it's lived.

Years ago, my family and I lived in the Bay Area of northern California. On the first Sunday morning we were in our new pastorate, our congregation consisted of one woman and her baby. With no congregation to speak of, there were no offerings to speak of, either. Some days we found ourselves eating oatmeal for breakfast, again for lunch, and again at the evening meal.

Slowly, the church grew as other families attended.

John and his family came, liked us, and stayed as part of the congregation all the time we lived and pastored there. He worked for the airlines nearby and was moderately successful financially. At least he was feeding his family a variety of foods, which was more than I could say for myself at the time.

But he was a talker rather than a doer. I'll never forget that Sunday as long as I live. It was after the morning worship when he slapped me on the back and said, "Pastor, if I had a million dollars, I'd be happy to give you a tithe of that. Or if I had a thousand, I'd give you a hundred. I know that would help."

I said nothing, but I thought plenty: "Brother, if you had ten, a dollar would help right now."

He gave nothing. His wife made a contribution to the church out of her meager grocery allowance from time to time. He was always going to do things or change his ways, but he never did. He was deceiving himself by thinking that talking about it was doing it.

Remember: change is not change until something is changed.

Giving is not giving until it's given.

Faith is not faith until it's action.

Not too long ago I saw John again, after almost thirty years. Still, there was no change. He was still a talker and not a doer. His value to the kingdom of God has never changed either. That's not the manhood God wants from us.

One of the concepts to come out of the "Me Decade" of the '70s was the concept of the "courage to create." The thought was not new, of course, except for the phraseology. The courage to create was suddenly recognized as a special boldness in those rare individuals who are willing to produce something original rather than just reproduce or duplicate something else.

Writers have often described the sense of nausea they feel as they roll a blank sheet of paper into the typewriter. With each fresh page, they must muster the courage to create.

Courage has always been a requirement of leadership.

"Be of good courage" is a scriptural refrain.

"Take courage." Angels used such commands as salutations. "Be of good cheer" really means to be of "good courage."

John Kennedy made a name for himself, before ever becoming president of the United States, with his book *Profiles in Courage*. And yet, profiles in courage are nothing new—not after you have read about Abraham, Joshua, Moses, David, Paul, and the other "heroes of the faith" in the Bible. Their exploits were such that the Scriptures state that *"the world was not worthy"* (Hebrews 11:38) of them.

Much of the modern church has failed to inspire, or require, courage in its men. Many pastors find they can preach to women, organize women, and work with women with much less effort than with men. In fact, many pastors today cannot relate to men in a positive way. It's the reason why women outnumber men by such a large margin in many churches, and why the matriarchal society is being perpetuated instead of the patriarchal.

Courage is the virtue, quality, or attribute of life that enables a man to face disapproval, persecution, fear, failure, and even death with a real manliness.

It takes courage to face reality.

Peter wrote, *"Add to your faith virtue"* (2 Peter 1:5). *"Virtue"* means moral excellence, manliness, courage.

Scripture recounts Joseph living in Potiphar's house and being tempted by Potiphar's wife's attempts to seduce him. It tells us that Joseph rebuked her, saying, *"How then can I do this great wickedness, and sin against God?"* (Genesis 39:9). The honor of God was the criteria of his life. That's manliness.

It takes courage to be a man.

I was the general manager of a television station when it came time to reduce personnel because of economic reasons. My son, Paul, was a program producer there, but others had more seniority. There came a time when a choice had to be made, and I called Paul in to talk to him

It takes courage to face reality.

and tell him what was happening. After hearing me out, he just looked at me, and then said something that made me realize what a real man he had become.

"Dad, let me go. I'll make it on my own."

He did.

It was hard for both of us; it required courage, but as I look back at it, that was the day that I realized his manhood.

Nehemiah, the three Hebrew children, Daniel, Joshua—Scripture is replete with those who added courage to their faith.

John the Baptist added courage to his faith, and having rebuked the king, was beheaded. But John knew, and others since then know, the principle.

Some things in life are more important than life itself.

Truth, honor, integrity, and other marks of a man require courage. Or love.

In San Diego, a man plunged into a house that was a roaring inferno because his child was still there. They both died. To him his child was more important than his own life.

Courage is necessary to change.

Many men today will change wives, children, businesses, anything, rather than change themselves. Real men face reality and change.

My associate, Jeremy, was pastoring in a New England town. His congregation wanted to remodel their building, feeling that it was necessary to attract people from the outside into their place of worship.

When Jeremy was praying about the remodeling, he became aware of something he had never known before. The Holy Spirit began to lead Jeremy into the Word and make him aware of certain Scriptures.

The first was, *"Delight yourself also in the LORD, and He shall give you the desires of your heart"* (Psalm 37:4); the second was, God is *"the author and finisher of our faith"* (Hebrews 12:2). With those two verses, Jeremy began to understand that God is the author of our desires. He doesn't just grant us the desires we have, but He authors His desires in us so that He can fulfill them. In that way, He can bring His kingdom to earth through us.

> **God authors His desires in us so we can fufill them and bring His kingdom to earth.**

From there, the next step was an understanding that the Lord really had put the desire to remodel in the hearts of the people, but the remodeling the Lord wanted was *in their hearts*. In their lack of spirituality, they had transferred their desire to the material and out of the realm of the Spirit.

CHANGING HEADS

Couples sense the need for change, but rather than changing in heart or mind, they simply change houses, and their problems remain. A man is sensitive to his need for change; but rather than asking God to change his heart, he changes jobs, and the old habits remain.

How many church buildings across the nation have been remodeled without benefit of growth or blessing, because the change needed was not in the building, but in the hearts of the people?

Do you sense your need for change? You're the man—you change, then your family will.

You change, then your business will.

The change begins in you first.

CHAPTER 10

THE BUCK STOPS HERE

God has planned for someone to take charge. Men, it is you. The Bible, in Ephesians 5:23, names the man as the head of the house, comparing him to Christ as the head of the church. It has a powerful meaning for men.

The truth: As Christ is the Savior of the church, and provides solutions to the problems of its members, so is the man to be toward his family. Solutions to family problems are to initiate with the man.

At the end of a meeting in Phoenix, Arizona, a couple approached me. She did the talking, and he stood a little behind and to one side of her.

"Our daughter," she said, "has run away from home. We want you to pray for us that God will bring her back."

"Well, I'll be happy to agree with you in prayer about that," I responded. I looked at her husband. "Do you have anything to say?" I asked.

"No," he replied, "I think she has said it all." So we prayed together. They returned a few hours later for the evening meeting, ahead of everyone else. When I arrived early myself, I found them waiting.

Their daughter was with them.

"Our daughter has just come home," the woman said, "but we can't seem to talk to her. She won't say much to us, but maybe she'll talk to you. Would you talk to her?"

I invited the girl to step into a small, nearby classroom with me. As the father of two girls, I had some paternal experience as well.

The young girl was thirteen years old, and she was nervous. I asked her a few simple questions. Her answers at first were monosyllabic.

"How do you like your mother?" I finally asked in the course of our conversation. The girl sparked somewhat when I asked that. Using the teenage version of eloquent, she told me about her mother.

"And how about Dad?"

She fell sullen and silent. I waited a moment, expecting at least some response. There was none.

"Is there something wrong with Dad?" I asked. She sat and looked out the window and gave no response. Not a word.

So we talked about other matters. At last, when she began telling me about a problem she had, I asked her why she didn't tell her father.

"He won't listen," she stated abruptly.

"What do you mean?" I asked her.

"He never listens," she responded. "When I try to tell him something or explain something to him, he won't listen. He never accepts my side of the argument, and he blames me for everything."

She had her momentum now. She went on, but the message was clear. I knew what her problem was.

In a few minutes, I brought her back to her parents. They looked at me expectantly.

"I've had a very nice talk with your daughter," I told them. "I think things can work out well."

The father said nothing. The mother waited a moment, then, looking nonplussed, asked, "Isn't there anything we need to *know?*"

"Yes," I answered. "Do you want your daughter to stay at home, and do you want to have a normal relationship with her?"

"Why, of course," the mother replied.

I looked straight at her and said, "Ma'am, I'm talking to your husband now."

That was startling for all of them.

"Okay," I told him. "I'll pray with you again and agree with you in prayer for your daughter. I'll pray that she will have a complete change of mind, heart, and attitude, and you will have a perfectly normal household." I looked at the three of them. "Are we agreed on that?" They all nodded.

"I'll do it under one condition, though," I said to him. "I'll agree with you in prayer for these things only if you agree with this one condition. Will you do it?"

He shifted uncomfortably. "I'm not sure I want to, until I hear it," he said.

"It's going to be your responsibility," I told him. "You're the one who's going to be responsible for the change in your daughter. Can you accept that responsibility?"

"Sure," he muttered.

"All right, here's the condition," I told him. "For the next thirty days, your daughter can say anything to you she wants to say, any time she wants to say it, and any way she wants to say it. And you can only listen to her. You can't answer her or anything until those thirty days are up. Then you can talk to her."

The father swallowed hard. He was stunned. Ridiculous. There was no way he could agree to something like that. Not in his own home.

"Fine," I shrugged. "Then I can't agree with you in prayer for a change of heart in your daughter and normal relationships in your household."

"What you're asking is impossible!" he protested.

"It is not impossible," I countered. "It is simply a question of whether or not you desire a change in your home—and whether you can be responsible for it."

Finally, caught between the proverbial rock and the hard place, he agreed weakly.

"I don't know if I can do it," he said, "but I'll try."

The four of us prayed together. I agreed with them for a complete change in their daughter—in her heart, mind, attitude, and affections.

Three months later, I found myself back in the city of Phoenix. I walked into that same church on a Sunday evening. The first ones to meet me were the father, mother, and daughter I had prayed with on my last trip.

They were a totally different family—outgoing, happy, standing close to each other, unafraid to touch one another.

"What happened to you?" I cried out when I saw them. "Evidently God answered prayer!"

"God really did answer prayer," the father said. "I listened, and then listened some more. At first it was all I could do to restrain myself from telling her I'd had it with her, grounding her for a month for what she was saying, and just really giving it to her. But I did remember that I wanted a change. So with all that was in me, and all that God could give me, I listened to her.

"Finally, as I listened, I began to realize that some of the things she was saying were right. I was wrong."

As it turned out, the condition had not been technically met. The experiment didn't last the whole thirty days.

"It lasted only about three weeks," the father explained. "That's when my daughter decided she had said everything she had wanted to say. She walked in and sat down on the edge of the bed one evening and said to me, 'I'm all finished for now. What do you want to say to me?'"

In that moment, the father told me, there was the beginning of a beautiful restoration in their relationship.

"My wife and I just reached out our arms, and she came to us. We hugged her and just loved her. When I began to talk to her, I told her how I had been wrong, recalling times when I had been brusque or abrupt, times when I had not listened to her side of the story, times when I had taken somebody else's side, times when I had put undue burdens on her, and times when she had done the same to us."

The man was glowing when he told me the story and the end result.

"When I asked my daughter to forgive me," he said, "that was the moment she began to change, and our whole family is changed today. My problem was the fact that I was so busy I didn't take time to listen to my daughter."

The daughter, it turned out, had not completely failed her family. The mother had become the leader only out of necessity. She was not the source of the breakdown in the family. It was the father's responsibility; he was responsible for the family's problem. He didn't listen, but when he began to listen, he became responsible for success in their relationships.

The solution to family problems, in God's order for the family, is to begin with the father.

Millions of men duplicate the effort (or lack of it) of that father in Phoenix. They are so occupied with their "busy-ness" that they leave the ministry of listening to the children in their wives' hands.

It is man abdicating part of his manhood.

It is a rare family these days where the man of the house exercises leadership in solving family problems. Passing the proverbial buck has become a fine art in this world.

President Harry Truman made himself a folk hero by planting a peculiar sign on his desk in the Oval Office. It declared, "The buck stops here." All the buck-passing stopped at his desk. Truman understood that tough truth as one of the marks of a leader.

Buck-passing is the colloquial term for self-justification. Justification—that theological tongue twister—simply means "being made right." On the other hand, self-justification means "making yourself right in your own eyes." It was in Eden that the pattern for self-justification was set, and it is still lived out today.

> **Men are so occupied with their "busy-ness" that they don't listen to their children.**

Adam sinned in Eden, and as a result, he hid himself from God. There came a moment when God called to Adam, and he had to come out of hiding. God's insistent inquiry as to his whereabouts caused Adam to explain his absence.

"I was afraid because I was naked; and I hid myself" (Genesis 3:10).

Guilt, fear, and hiding—the sequentially ordered results of sin established millenniums ago in Eden—are still the same today.

No man can live with guilt. It is a killer. Guilt weighs heavily and leads to fear.

So men still hide. They try to escape. Escape reality. Escape God. Escape responsibility. They do it by using philosophy, drugs, alcohol, pleasure, and many other things.

But getting rid of guilt by any of these methods is just being made right in your own eyes. Self-justification is buck-passing. Read how Adam did it, and you will see the "how-to" pattern for trying to get rid of guilt that he set for all men, from the days in the Garden until now.

"Did you take of the tree?" God asked Adam.

"The woman made me do it."

Place the blame on someone else. It's easy to do. Take your guilt, give it to another by putting the blame on him, and you are free! Just pass the buck.

Note how well Eve learned from Adam. When she was asked if she had taken the fruit of the tree, her reply was according to pattern.

"The Devil made me do it," she pouted.

Flip Wilson, the comedian, made millions of dollars and millions of people laugh with that line, but it wasn't funny in reality.

Eve made herself right in her own eyes by placing the blame on the Devil. However, all she had demonstrated was that all sin does originate with Satan, but hers was a wrong use of the truth.

Truth is the foundation for life, but blackmail is one misuse of the truth. It's wrong. So was Eve. So are those today who practice the same pattern of self-justification.

Consider the ingrained process in the man sitting at his breakfast table at home. His wife is fixing something at the sink, and his son sits with him at the table. The son reaches for the toast, spills his milk, and looks quickly at his father. The father scowls, scolds, and slaps.

"How many times do I have to tell you to watch what you're doing?" the father asks. No answer is needed. As the son cries, the father and mother clean the table.

Now, it's a week later, with the same family at the same breakfast table. Father reaches for the toast. His elbow spills the glass of milk. The son looks quickly and intently at the father to see what will happen this time.

Father scowls at mother. Then he speaks to her.

"How many times do I have to tell you," he demands, "not to put the milk so close to my elbow?"

Dad justified himself by placing the blame on someone else. In so doing, he taught his son by example to do likewise.

That behavioral trench is dug deep in the soil of the human soul. Its ruts run to ruin. Men today practice as a science what Adam and Eve practiced as a desperate experiment. Modern man blames the woman as if that is the way it should be.

Wrong.

> **Every man must answer to God for his own actions.**

Every man must answer for his own actions, and he must answer to God alone. That is why Calvary, where Christ died, is so important. It is the only place in the world where sin can be placed and forgiveness from God received. It is the only place where guilt can be released.

Tragic consequences are left on society by men who still try to cover their mistakes, errors, and sins. Think of those who would rather let their marriages die than to admit their sins and give their relationships new life. Men who would rather let their businesses collapse than confront failure and give their work new life. Men who would rather let their children flee in frustration than come to grips with their own shortcomings and renew those ragged relationships.

When a man fails to confess his own sins, when he steps into the background and allows problems to swallow up the members of his family, he is actually a coward.

There are times when silence is golden; other times, it is just plain yellow.

> **God looks to the man for strong family leadership.**

God looks to the man for strong family leadership.

I have a close personal friend whom we'll call Jerry.

Jerry's youngest daughter, Cheryl, as a teenager, rebelled against the lifestyle of her parents, and became very willful, independent, and rebellious.

She did her own thing, with or without the blessing of her parents. In her many escapades, there always seemed to be a boy involved. Her parents worried about her.

A pattern of behavior evolved: escapade, punishment, reconciliation. Again and again, we saw the scene played out in living color.

One day Cheryl disappeared.

For almost two full days, her anxious parents searched for her, called relatives, inquired discreetly among neighbors, and questioned her friends. Though they did not want to involve the police, finally they had no choice. She had been gone too long, and it would be dangerous not to call the authorities.

But news travels fast on the teenage grapevine. The moment the decision was made to call the police, Cheryl's cooperating friends alerted her. Within the hour, she was back home. She had been at a friend's house not too far away.

But news had gotten out, the police had been called, and now everyone knew about their problem.

Jerry vowed to punish his daughter. He was determined to humiliate her as she had the family. I knew his attitude, because I had been with him through the whole ordeal. I knew what he was suffering as a man and as a father. He was embarrassed, and he was determined to make her feel what he felt.

What he did not realize was that the discipline he was planning for his daughter was not only for correction, but also for revenge.

That would harden her, not change her.

I knew I had to minister to him. He was the one who needed it now, so I invited him to go with me to a coffee shop. It was going to be just him and me, eyeball-to-eyeball, man-to-man.

"You know what's happening to you?" I asked over coffee, after our preliminary remarks. "You're resentful because you think your daughter has taken away your prestige in the community, undermined your position in the church, and tarnished your reputation as a man and father. You're thinking that because of her you're suffering a loss of status."

He was staring at me, but I went ahead for his own good. He was my friend.

"In the first place, the truth is that almost everyone goes through these same things with their children. Maybe not precisely like you have, but similarly, in lots of ways. So the people that you think are looking at you critically aren't. What they're really looking at is your reaction. They're looking at you to see how you handle this whole thing.

"Right now, Cheryl's getting sympathy because of your actions, instead of suffering because of hers."

He didn't say a word. He just looked at me.

"You're the one suffering," I told him, "and you're taking it out on her. What you need to do is to forgive her again, love her, and try to communicate with her. Ask God what to do and say. How can you communicate with her when you're condemning her? Christ said that He did not come to condemn, but to save (John 3:17). You're the one who needs to ask God for the solution. Besides, as the head of your house, you're the one who is responsible for initiating the effort to find the solution. When you change, she'll start changing."

There was more, but that is the substance of what I said. I didn't see him for several days. When we did meet again, we headed for the coffee shop.

He sat there for a while, coffee cup in hand, and I just waited.

"After you said what you did," he began, "I thought a lot about it, and I decided you were wrong. But then, the more I examined my motives, actions, and what I had said, the more I began to think that maybe you were partially right."

I waited, listening.

"Late that night, after we talked," he continued, "I went out into our backyard, where I do my private praying. It came to me, while I was there, that no matter what caused Cheryl's rebellion, it was up to me to provide a solution, or at least begin to try to find one."

He said that, as he walked up and down in that backyard praying, alone with God, he found himself asking God for forgiveness for himself, for a renewal of his heart and mind, and for a clear passageway through which solutions could come. God changed his heart that night.

The transformation in his family began in that precious, private hour. Ensuing days would reveal openly what had happened in secret between a man and his Lord.

The rift between the father and daughter was bridged. The wounds were healed. Tension softened once again into affection. The solution came.

Father finally knew best.

Men have to learn to see themselves in the sight of God before they can see their families.

But no one can see a thing with the lights out. In a dark room, trying to walk around, you can bump into everything there and never know what you hit. Turn on the light, though, and it becomes clear. You can walk safely through it all.

The man who is spiritually dark can't see the nose on the front of his spiritual face. Jesus is the *"light of the world"* (John 8:12). In the light of His Word, we see ourselves. The Holy Spirit illumines the truth, and the truth makes us free (verse 32). God's Word is truth, and His Spirit is the Spirit of truth.

> **Men have to learn to see themselves in the sight of God before they see their families.**

God is not indifferent to our needs. It was for this purpose that Jesus Christ said He came into this world. It is the men who say they have no needs for whom God can do nothing. God loves you. God wants your good. God wants your life to be lived to the maximum.

Just as Jesus Christ is the head of the church and brings His salvation and solutions, He can do the same through you to your family. You are the channel. Your family looks to you first.

To try to escape from that responsibility is to hide from God. To refuse to acknowledge the need is to escape reality.

God is looking to you, as a man, to provide leadership. God has given His Word. And by His own Spirit, He has given the perfect tool: divine wisdom. With the Word and wisdom, He expects you to find the solutions.

Such is the challenge of manhood: to know God, to know yourself and your family, and to let the buck stop with you.

CHAPTER 11

VIDEO DADDY

Bart Simpson's cartoon dad Homer, foolish, weak, bumbling, is outsmarted by his loud-mouthed son before television viewers. Homer is the picture of manhood for millions of American children.

Ed Bundy on *Married with Children* is the ultimate incompetent father. He's a drunk and a lazy, perverted slob whose world revolves around himself and his ridiculous ideas of how to get rich quick. Yet even this sitcom seems morally tame compared to new award-winning series that laud homosexuality and the homosexual lifestyle.

In their perversion, these form an image of manhood that is stamped in the minds of millions in our country.

The images in our minds create the motivations for our behavior. We become the images we have of ourselves, and we treat others according to the images we have of them.

The most powerful thing that can be done in life is to create an image; the next most powerful thing is to destroy an image. Television has been creating and destroying images of manhood for decades, with dangerous results.

Our youth have been traumatized by the "video daddy." Ed Bundy, like it or not, is an example of an authority figure in the home. He and other foolish male characters more numerous to mention have distorted the image of husbands and fathers.

In its perversion, an image of manhood is stamped on the minds of our youth that results in their resentment, derision, anarchy, and mockery.

An exasperated father sat across from me and asked in frustration, "What's a man to do?"

His son was becoming a real problem. He thought he had been a good father and provided all the necessities of life. He just could not understand his son's attitude.

The most powerful thing that can be done in life is to create an image.

After a long conversation, it became very clear that this father was only one of thousands of men in our world today who have been *victimized* by forces they should have *controlled*.

What this father needed to understand was the power of images. It was his responsibility to exercise some kind of control over the images that were set before his son. By permitting his son to watch anything and everything on television, he was allowing other forces to create an image of authority in his son's mind.

Those TV caricatures became modern-day role models. Then, when the son saw a flaw, prejudice, or weakness in his father, he identified him with the image stamped on his mind via television. He transferred the image of a "Homer Simpson" to his own father, and then reacted with the same resentment or disdain that he had for the authority figure on the program.

Some parents remain perplexed over their children's behavior, until they understand the power of television. Others do understand. That is why some groups fight TV programming so vehemently.

Remember, the motive behind such television programming is the love of money, which is the root of all evil.

When confronted with the issue of TV influence, television producers deny such power over the minds of people. Yet out of the other side of their mouths, they sell thirty seconds of viewing time to sponsors for $300,000, assuring them that commercials will convince viewers to buy the products displayed. They can't have it both ways. Television either is or it isn't that powerful.

> **Television has distorted our image of husbands and fathers.**

It is.

The nation as a whole has been adversely affected by the video images of television programming. America has been going through a transition for the last few decades. The national image as a "virtuous" nation, a benefactor to the entire world, a savior from enslaving dictatorships, has undergone severe changes as a result of television. The destruction of those positive images in the national mentality has created a philosophical and emotional sickness in the nation's life.

Our youth have been specifically affected by it.

One of the most subtle catastrophes has been the "anti-hero" syndrome that has eliminated our heroes and left us bereft of role models as patriotic examples.

There is a proverb that says, "God hates those who say that bad is good and good is bad." Yet that perversion has taken place covertly and overtly for the past decades.

The hero image in the mind of a young man powerfully motivates him in life. The hero image in a young girl's mind of the man she will someday marry also motivates her. Throughout life, there is a constant adjustment of the ideal and the real. The distance between the ideal and the real is the degree of disappointment in life. But our youth still need positive ideals and heroes who can affect them for good.

How can we change the negative, anti-hero images? By letting God renew the images in our minds.

Today, more than ever before in history, men need to recognize how God originally made them to be, and earnestly endeavor to let God recreate their manhood in the image of Christ.

> **How can we change the negative images? By letting God renew our minds.**

Adam was created in the image of God. His was the example of manhood. When that manhood was marred by sin, Jesus Christ came as the Second Adam to restore the image to men once again. Christ came as the *"express image"* (Hebrews 1:3) of God, to reveal His grace and truth.

As Jesus revealed the glory of God, He told us that we could be *"born again"* and receive the very nature of God into our spirits. We could have our minds renewed and our hearts regenerated. From there, our entire lives would be so changed that old things would pass away and all things would become new. Without Jesus Christ, man is unable to be restored to the image of God as *"His workmanship, created in Christ Jesus for good works"* (Ephesians 2:10). With Jesus, it is being done today.

With the new image of manhood—given by Jesus—stamped on our minds, our behavior, attitudes, and desires all become new. We are new creations with new motivations.

While I was in Cleveland's Hopkins Airport one day, I ran into a noted Christian author and lecturer. We spent a moment or two renewing our acquaintance. At the time, the ministry of "majoring in men" was just getting started, and I mentioned it to him.

He was vitally interested. He had just spoken to hundreds of men at a meeting in Cleveland.

He explained the text of Scripture that had greatly impressed him. He had used it to address those men because he believed it was a cornerstone for men today.

> **It's time for the Lord to turn the hearts of the fathers to the sons.**

"It's time for the Lord to turn the hearts of the fathers to the sons, and the sons to the fathers," he paraphrased from Malachi 4:6.

"We've had enough of the humanistic efforts to degrade men and breed contempt for fathers in the hearts of their sons.

"We need to speak loud and clear, and I'm glad you are doing it," he shared with me as we parted company for our respective planes.

The psalmist wrote: *"I will try to walk a blameless path, but how I need your help, especially in my own home, where I long to act as I should. Help me to refuse the low and vulgar things; help me to abhor all crooked deals of every kind, to have no part in them. I will reject all selfishness and stay away from every evil. I will not tolerate anyone who secretly slanders his neighbors; I will not permit conceit and pride. I will make the godly of the land my heroes, and invite them to my home. Only those who are truly good shall be my servants. But I will not allow those who deceive and lie to stay in my house"* (Psalm 101:2–7 TLB).

That sounds to me like God gave every Christian father a guide to take care of the "video daddy."

Christian television programming is one process by which millions are making the godly of the land their heroes and inviting them into their homes.

I'm the chairman of a group called the Committee for International Good Will. Our goal is to make the godly of the land our heroes. Annually, we conduct a banquet and honor one of the godly of the land as our "Man of the Year."

I formed the committee because I was just plain sick and tired of the world system creating the ungodly as heroes, making the bad good, and the good bad.

> **Every man has three functions in the home and community. He is to guide, guard, and govern.**

You need to form yourself as a committee of one in your home to do the same. Make the godly of the land your heroes. God says it, and by doing it you will create a positive image in the minds of your family, and their motivations will become right.

It is the aim of all *"seducing spirits, and doctrines of devils"* (1 Timothy 4:1 KJV) to demean, denigrate, and debilitate your manhood, to sap your Christian virility. In so doing, they cause the power of Christ to have little effect in your life. Reject such spirits and doctrines. Cast them from your home and family.

Every man has three functions in the home and community. He is to guide, guard, and govern. It is what God gave Adam to do on earth, and He has never rescinded that mantle of authority. If you are a man, it's yours. Wear it, and live it.

But wait a minute. The "video daddy" can also be an absentee father.

The greatest addiction in America is not marijuana, cocaine, or pills. It is television.

The absentee father today is often one who goes to work, comes home, and then sits in front of the television, forcing his wife and children into unnatural roles and responsibilities.

In Pittsburgh, sitting over a cup of coffee, a man told me something that made me proud to be his friend.

"I used to be one of those guys you preach to," he said. "I was a real television addict. But one day I realized what was happening and thought I needed to change. It wasn't until you came along, though, and hit me right between the eyes with it that I made the decision to do something about it.

"I talked with my wife, and we agreed to put the TV in the closet and bring it out only when the entire family agreed the program was something that we could all watch together, or that would be beneficial for one of us.

"I tell you, I had withdrawal symptoms," he laughed. "I don't know what it is like to stop drugs cold turkey. All I know is that it was bad enough with television. But let me tell you this. Since that time, my kids' grades have gone from D's to straight B's or better. I know more about them now, and we have the greatest time in the world just going places and doing things together.

"I've even taken them to the museum! We have done more things together since that television has been gone than we did in all our lives before that. It has been great!"

I received a call the other day in my kitchen at home. It was a minister's wife desperately concerned about her husband. He refused to take the leadership role in the church, forcing her to do it. The men didn't like it, and their wives were upset about it. But he was content to watch television between sermons.

That may be an isolated case, but it's a real one.

The "video daddy" on television, or the one in front of it—which is worse?

The best daddy is the one who uses the television to make the godly of the land his heroes.

Are there godly men left in our land? Despite all that television has said to the contrary, there are. But America's image still has a long way to go to be maximized.

> **The best daddy is the one who uses the television to make the godly of the land his heroes.**

Today, many men believe that America is great because of the virtue of its wealth. But it was the virtues of American men and women that brought us our wealth. Men, families, and nations are great by the wealth of their virtues, not by virtue of their wealth.

Men produce nations. A nation is great because its men are great.

For America to recapture its greatness, its men must recapture their manhood.

I attended a banquet one evening where the speaker related an incident that made an impact on everyone.

He said, "While I was at the airport today, someone very kindly commended me for my courage in talking on television about the American Civil Liberties Union, and how they are trying to destroy Christianity in America.

"He told me that, some years ago, he had rebuked them publicly on his own television program. When they retaliated, he dropped the matter because he said 'he had too much to lose.'

"Too much to lose?" the speaker raised his voice. "What have we got to lose? I started this entire ministry with seventy dollars, and I have a hundred now, so what have I got to lose?"

The applause started as a ripple but became a river of appreciation.

Manhood is measured in spirit. It has nothing to do with physical size, but everything to do with character.

Modern youth need fathers of good courage.

They need heroes. They need Joshuas who will cry, *"As for me and my house, we will serve the Lord"* (Joshua 24:15). They need Daniels who will face the legal lions of our day and shut their mouths from speaking pompous words against God.

E. M. Bounds wrote, *"Men are God's methods."*

While men look for better methods, God looks for better men. God is looking for them right now. What about you?

CHAPTER 12

OUR FATHER, WHICH ART INACTIVE

Men have long striven to give their children a better life than they had. They establish trusts and college funds; they pull strings behind the scenes to get jobs for their children; they pave the way however they can.

But the material things, in the long run, may mean little. Nothing substitutes for example. The child needs a father, not a guardian angel. The child comes equipped with a guardian angel as a standard feature. But to have a real father should also be a standard feature, not a luxury option.

The greatest thing a father can do for his children is to love their mother.

I have been far from the perfect parent. I wish I had a better track record to report. But once I began to make Nancy my joint heir, to appreciate rather than depreciate her, parenting became a less tumultuous effort.

But parenting is still life's greatest art form.

Today, my son, Paul, is one of America's leading Christian television producers. But the day he kicked a hole in the door, we both could have become losers.

That was the day we both learned the meaning of courage.

Life and death are in our decisions.

My daughter, Lois, marched through law school and passed the bar with a flourish. Today, she is a deputy district attorney in Orange County, California. But there was a day when Lois's future hinged on my willingness to make the right decision.

For five years I had been the president of a denominational laymen's organization, with five thousand men and four thousand boys under my care and leadership. The job required ceaseless travel, absences from home, and I spent much of my time ministering "on the road."

> **The greatest thing a father can do for his children is to love their mother.**

Nancy welcomed me home one day with a tense expression on her face. Lois seemed to be slipping away. She had always been an exceedingly popular girl, always in the social limelight. But now she was letting the peer pressure get to her and affect her attitude and behavior. She was getting involved with friends who did not hold to the same standards of Christian life that we held in our home.

I looked at my job. I loved it. The nationwide travel and speaking engagements suited me fine.

And yet my daughter needed a father.

I did not know then what I know now: that today's society is suffering from absent fathers.

Nancy and I agreed that it would be best if I were home more consistently. I resigned my position, accepted the pastorate of a church, and settled in to become more of a full-time father.

It was a quality decision. And the right one.

Today, Lois is a deep-rooted, exuberant Christian woman, married, the mother of a beautiful baby—and a very successful attorney.

My younger daughter, Joann, is a missionary to Japan, teaching English and the Bible. She graduated summa cum laude from college, and soon after, she accepted God's will for her life to serve Him in Japan.

Nancy and I thank the Lord for our children and how they are today. I wish I could take credit for them, but I really have to give it to the Lord, their mother, and friends.

Friends.

Earl Book is a friend. While I was with him in Albany, Oregon, many years ago, Earl gave me a piece of wisdom that I have never forgotten; I made it a real part of my family's life.

> **I determined to have as many godly people in my house as possible.**

While I was with him, I could not help but notice his children, their demeanor, attitude, manners, and spirit. I lauded Earl for the great work of fathering them that he had obviously done.

"I can't really take much credit for my children," he said humbly. "I learned a powerful truth from a couple who were with me in a missionary convention. They had a tremendous effect on my children. After they left, my children were still being influenced by the visit of that couple.

"I realized at that time what a potent influence others are on my children. I determined right then to have as many godly people in my home as possible, so their influence would take effect on my children."

Earl was too humble. His own godly influence was a major factor, I'm sure. Yet the lesson he shared influenced me to make an effort to do the same with my children. I believe the success of that endeavor is obvious today.

The modern American father thinks all too often that fathering is paying the bills, providing a home and education, allowing recreation, administering an occasional lecture, and, at various times and in varying degrees, being the disciplinarian.

But fathering is a comprehensive task. It requires maximized manhood.

It means thinking, studying, monitoring, recommending, influencing, and loving. Remember, love is the desire to benefit others even at the expense of self because love desires to give. Lust desires to benefit self even at the expense of others because lust desires to get. This is true in the home, business, and in every circumstance.

> **The dinner hour is one of the most important hours in a child's life.**

Even at supper.

For years we have known that young people learn to have good interpersonal relationships from their encounters at the dinner table in their homes. The dinner hour is one of the most important hours in a child's life. It's the hour that is made for listening, as well as for sharing the hurts, pains, victories, and blessings of the day. It is a time for learning to communicate.

But many of today's men minimize this opportunity. They lose valuable time that needs to be spent as quality time with the family. It is a tragedy in the American home today that instead of utilizing the dinner hour to establish relationships and strengthen ties in the family, it is squandered.

Jesus said in John 10:10, *"The thief does not come except to steal, and to kill, and to destroy."*

Much of television is like a thief. It steals time, it kills initiative, and it destroys relationships.

Watching the news on television during the dinner hour can wreak havoc in the home. Children who spend their dinner hour watching crime, war, disaster, divorce, and tragedy are themselves victimized, even traumatized.

Instead of the father allaying fears, giving comfort, imputing truth, healing hurts, or bringing encouragement during the dinner hour, he lets negative factors cause disturbance, disorientation, and displeasure to his children.

One father I know complained about his daughter not having an appetite, never wanting to eat at home, but always eating heartily when dining out in a restaurant. What he needed to know was that there was no television when they were dining out. He thought she was only trying to spend his money. She wasn't.

While speaking at a men's retreat at Hume Lake, California, I made the tragic statement that the average American father gives only three minutes per day of quality time to his child. After the session ended, one of the men challenged me on my facts.

"You preachers just say things," he chided. "The latest study shows that the average American father does not give three minutes per day, but only *thirty-five seconds of undivided attention* to his child each day."

I accepted that because he was the superintendent of schools for the central California area. In fact, he gave me another startling statistic.

In a California school district, there were four hundred and eighty-three students in a "continuation" program. That's the program for students who need help in school. Out of that number of students, *not one* had a father at home.

In one school district on the outskirts of Seattle, 61 percent of the children have no father at home!

The absentee father is the curse of our day.

And it may well be that the father is home every day but does not spend time with his children. Corporate life with its pressures to produce loyalty to the logo and affection for ambition create havoc in the home. Many wives know that their husbands' adulterous relationships are not with other women, but with their jobs. Other men hide in their hobbies.

Quality time is when the family eats together, prays together, shares friends together. The prayer that produces intimacy between a man and a woman does the same in the family.

The man is the leader.

Leading his family in righteousness is his prime responsibility and priestly ministry. To abandon it for personal pleasure, forfeit it through moral cowardice, or shirk it because of irresponsibility is a sin. Sin.

The father's noblest action is giving himself to his children and to God.

The true legacy of the father is in the spirit he gives his children. *Trust funds can never be a substitute for a fund of trust.*

Active fathers who lead their children into a strong relationship with God and family maximize their own manhood.

CHAPTER 13

STOP, LOOK, LISTEN

One of the most successful insurance men on the West Coast stood up to address a very sophisticated, urbane group of people—an insurance brokers' convention in San Jose. He had been promoted as a "super salesman," and the air was keen with excitement and anticipation. "Super salesman" was about to tell his secrets.

When at last he stood to speak, he was disappointing to look at after all the talk about him. He had a rather rumpled look. He stood relaxing against the corner of a table, one hand stuck in his pocket, with his tie slightly askew.

Yet this man had sold more insurance than anyone in the room.

"You know, I don't have much to say," he began slowly, sounding something like the late Will Rogers. "I'll take only a few minutes. I know everyone has talked about how much insurance I've sold. But when I started in this business a few years ago, I had a friend who was really successful, and he gave me a bit of advice. And all I've ever done is just follow that advice."

Everyone seemed to lean forward, waiting for an eloquent truth of motivational theory.

"What my friend told me was this," the speaker continued. "'You can get a man to do anything you want him to, if only you listen to him long enough.' So when I go to talk with someone, I listen to him. And after I've listened long enough, I simply say, 'Okay, why don't you just sign right here?' And he does. When you've asked enough questions and listened to someone long enough, it's your turn to speak, and all you do is ask for his signature."

With that he sat down.

Some are talkers. Others are listeners. The one who listens before he talks will succeed.

All this salesman did was to set forth in his own idiom a basic and primitive sales principle. That is, listen until you hear what the need is, and then simply meet the need.

> **Listen until you hear what the need is, and then simply meet the need.**

A wife has a need, and a man listens until he hears it. Listening is not a random function of the auditory members of your body.

Listening is ministry.

Over and over again through His Word, God says, *"He who has an ear, let him hear."* God places a premium on listening.

That father whom I instructed to listen silently to his daughter for thirty days learned the hard way that listening is a key to a father's ministry in the home. When I laid down the condition, the man told me later, he never came so close to hitting a preacher in his life. But the strange experiment proved the point: *men must learn to listen.*

The Bible tells us to study the Word of God to show ourselves approved. As men, we must study our wives and our children, and do it in the light of God's Word. We must listen to them in order to learn from them as a first basic step toward ministering to them.

A recent poll showed startling facts. Seventy-five percent of the men told pollsters their marriages were all right. Twenty-five percent of the wives of those same men said their marriages were all right.

That left fifty percent of the men with problems in their marriages, and they didn't even realize it! Why? They had not listened to their wives. They had not studied their marriage partners. They had not educated themselves in the uniqueness of their wives, their needs, their inner longings, their satisfaction thresholds.

Large corporations are spending untold thousands of dollars these days simply to teach their executives to listen. Without the listening skill, it's impossible to locate needs.

I have counseled people for thousands of hours in my life—fighting sleep through much of it, I'm afraid. But counseling is just glorified listening, for the most part, until the person has talked through the strata of life and begins to explore areas never before brought to light. Like the award-winning salesman, the counselor must listen long enough to find the need.

The man of the house is a leader, steward, priest, minister-counselor. He must be everything to his home that Christ is to the church.

No small job description.

That's why it takes a man.

And that's why you need to be maximized in your manhood.

Men and women are different. Really different.

For example, men are headliners; women are fine print people.

I flew across the continent and then drove for hours to see my brand-new granddaughter in the hospital. When I saw her, I checked her out thoroughly.

There she was—arms, legs, eyes, nose, mouth. All the parts were there; everything was okay. That was sufficient for me. I was ready to leave.

Not my wife and daughter. Half an hour later, they were still examining the length of the eyelashes, the shape of the fingernails, the texture of the skin, as if the nursery window were a magnifying glass.

Fine print, fine print.

The man comes home from work. His wife says, "How did it go today?"

"All right."

"What did you do?"

"Worked."

"Did you sell anything?"

"Yeah."

"What did you sell?"

"Contract to Sears."

"The one you have been working on for six months?"

"Yeah."

"You mean we're going to get a commission?"

"Yeah."

"How much?"

"I don't know. For Pete's sake, stop asking so many questions!"

She wants the fine print; all he's giving her are the headlines.

But the fine print is part of ministering. She needs to know. To minister to her, you have to give her some fine print.

What the man in the conversation was doing was committing the sin of omission.

The sin of omission is the basic sin of humanity.

The only reason you do wrong is *because you don't do right*.

I heard an evangelist telling some people that they would go to hell if they did certain things, such as get drunk, commit adultery, and other such acts. But people are not heading into an eternity without God because of what they do; it's because of what they don't do.

The sinner goes to hell for something he didn't do: he didn't believe on the Lord Jesus Christ and receive Him as his personal Savior. That sin of omission—not believing and receiving Jesus—is the basis of eternal separation from God.

Having not been born again—not receiving the Spirit of Jesus Christ into his life—a man winds up committing all kinds of transgressions and repetitive sins. That basic principle has eternal significance and consequences.

> **The sin of omission is doing wrong because you fail to do what is right.**

But the sin of omission is also a daily one, one that dogs you continually until you do something about it.

Women's frustrations with men are not because of what they do, but because of what they don't do. Husbands don't get in trouble when they fix the screen door, or fix the leaky faucet, but when they don't do it.

If we made all the right decisions and did all the right things every moment of the day, we'd never do anything wrong. But by failing to fill our minds with godly thoughts and divine truths, failing to meditate on that which is true, a thousand fragments of filth will swarm in.

Every man must fight the sin of omission. He must minister to his family by listening to each of them. He needs to develop the art of listening to know what their needs are so that he can help meet them.

Communication is the basis of life. When communication stops, abnormality sets in. The ultimate end of such abnormality, when it is not corrected, is death to the relationship. That is why I want to repeat my warning about the abuse of television.

A man cannot hear the needs of his family when he is listening to the demands of the TV. Nor can his family learn healthy communication through casual exchanges, made while sitting beside an impersonal television set.

Today, there is a new movement afoot.

It is the movement of the "maximized man."

Families are finding themselves again, Dad is listening again, lost members are being rediscovered right in the home, and old loves are being rekindled. Parents are reuniting emotionally with their children; relationships are being reestablished; children are learning to interact with adults once again.

It is an amazing transformation.

I walked into a building in Texas to get ready for the lecture and ministry of the evening. The place was packed with people. During the message, I talked about the "maximized man" with the darkened television set.

A young, energetic, personable young man walked up to me after the meeting, smiling cheerfully, and with hand held out for me to shake.

"I just have to tell you," he said, "that last Saturday night I took care of my television set.

"But I did it in a different way. I didn't just turn it off. I took it across the street and put it in a dumpster. You can't believe how good I have felt since then, or how good my family and I are getting along in just a few days."

As the leader, steward, priest, minister, counselor, you must have the courage to be the man your family wants you to be. Stop and listen to their needs. Then you will be the man God wants you to be, too.

CHAPTER 14

BORN-AGAIN MARRIAGE

How did you happen to marry your wife?" I asked a man not long ago. "She was the sister of a friend of someone I went on a blind date with one time," he shrugged.

Obviously his destiny.

"Why did you marry your wife?" I asked another.

"I was following a military parade down the street, and someone grabbed me and kissed me, and later I married her."

A patriotic partnership, if nothing else.

"Why did you marry?" I queried a young lady.

"I couldn't wait to get away from home," she replied directly. "My parents were unbearable. I married the first man I dated."

I wondered if he knew that.

The list of reasons is long, varied, and often sad. One man represented thousands of others when he told me at a men's retreat that he and his wife had engaged in premarital sex. She had become pregnant, and both sets of parents, plus their own consciences, caused the marriage.

I've watched couples agonize for hours in counseling sessions before they can confront and confess the truth about their motives for marriage. As it often turns out, the marriage commitment is deeply flawed because of something in the past.

Either the husbands or wives do not really believe that their partners were God's perfect choices for them, or they harbor a grudge for some wrong their partners did to them long ago. So the foundation of the marriage is not a solid rock, but rather a quagmire of hurts, misunderstandings, suspicions, resentment, and guilt.

> **Often marriage is flawed because husbands or wives don't believe their partner was God's perfect choice for them.**

Marriage can be the closest thing to a heaven or a hell that many will find on this earth.

Tim and Alice came to me for counseling. They were suffering in their marriage, even though he was a minister. Because of that, he felt ashamed to disclose anything about himself, or have his wife say anything about him.

Her pain in mind and spirit was obvious.

His discomfort at being there was also obvious.

He had come from a "macho" family where the man ruled everything. His father and brothers were uncouth and crude; much of their conduct was licentious and profane. However, Tim had come under the influence of the Word of God and to the revelation of soul that Jesus Christ was his personal Savior. He repented of his sins, believed on the Lord, and became a new person when the Spirit of God came into his life in saving power.

Because of the great grace God had shown him, the joy of knowing his sins were forgiven, and the desire to share the Good News with as many others as possible, he enrolled in a Bible college.

Alice, on the other hand, was a typical preacher's kid. Reared on the front pew, she had never known anything but a Christian life and culture. She, like Tim, wanted to share her love for Jesus with the whole world, and, as expected, enrolled in Bible college to equip herself for that mission.

They met in college.

They dated for a year, and the day finally came when she accepted his proposal; they announced their engagement.

Three weeks before the wedding date, they were together in an isolated area. Embracing her, Tim became more passionate than she was comfortable with, but she could not seem to stop his advances. He pressed the issue according to the old standards of a home that did not have a biblical basis for right and wrong.

His rationale: they would be married in three weeks anyway, so why wait? She knew better, but not wanting to displease him, she acquiesced.

They had sex in the back room of an old building.

Six years later, they were in my office.

Their lives, while publicly affectionate, were privately volatile. Harsh words, bitter accusations, even physical violence resulted from unresolved issues, unforgiven deeds, and unfulfilled love.

He complained of her latent hostility.

She criticized his lack of manhood toward her.

Through the hours of guiding them from thought to thought and feeling to feeling, we struck bedrock. Finally, after six years of marriage, she brought herself to say what had been repressed all those years.

She resented Tim for not allowing her to be a virgin when they married.

Face-to-face with the issue, Tim looked at her with a mixture of amazement and anger.

"Do you mean to tell me that you are blaming me for all the problems we have? Blaming me because of that one thing. I didn't even know it meant that much to you!" he exploded.

I cut into the conversation.

"Sir, that's exactly where it belongs—on you. Unless you accept your responsibility for your wife's sense of loss and shame, unless you ask forgiveness for that very thing, you will never have a right relationship with her."

He stormed out. Livid. But as he thought it through at home, he began to see how important it was to her, that he had robbed her of what she considered her most priceless gift to him. The sordid act in that back room was more like rape to her than the highest act of physical love between a man and a woman.

Eventually, the time came when he could confess that it was his lust, not his love, that had caused the problem. It was his fault, his sin, and he repented of it, asking forgiveness of his wife and making restitution to her. She genuinely forgave him. Her hostility was gone, and their lives changed dramatically.

It always amuses me when I see those old late-night movies where boy chases girl, then girl chases boy, and finally they get their misunderstandings cleared up. With a kiss, they pledge their troth at the altar. As they stand there, embracing at the outset of their marriage, just before the credits roll, these words become superimposed on the screen, "The End."

Anybody knows that is only the beginning and not the end.

There is a life principle based on Scripture that says it is harder to maintain than it is to obtain.

Jesus not only gives us life principles, but also the enabling power to live according to those principles.

Jesus Christ is not just the Savior of the soul, but the Savior of our total lives. Because ministers often talk about people as souls, or because the translation of Scripture refers to men as souls, it has not been uncommon for men to think that Jesus is only the Savior of the soul.

Jesus is *the* Savior. Your Savior.

Jesus is the Savior of your soul, your marriage, your emotions, your mind, your job, your education, your children.

You need Jesus for every area of your life.

You need Jesus for the totality of your life.

Betty grew up in a Christian home. Bill became a born-again believer in a Bible-believing church when he was thirteen. The two of them met at youth meetings, and they were married when he was eighteen and she was sixteen.

Bill became a very successful businessman over the years. Betty

> **You need Jesus for every area of your life—for the totality of your life.**

developed into an extremely popular, vivacious young woman, an active wife and mother of two. They were the model family, involved in the affairs of business, community, and church.

They were looked upon as exemplary leaders and pointed to as a pattern for other young couples.

Fifteen years into the marriage, tension was running high. Behind closed doors, Bill and Betty were locked into a cold war. They wanted a change, needed a change, but couldn't find it.

During that time I was teaching a leadership training course on the characteristics of Christlikeness. My thesis then and now is that true manhood is Christlikeness. These words imprinted themselves upon Bill's mind, and he meditated on them.

Inevitably, another crisis occurred at home. Betty fiercely accused her husband, telling him what she thought he was really like. After a long, heated exchange, Bill burst out of the house and headed for the car.

Once inside the car, with the door slammed shut, he put his head down on the steering wheel and clenched his fists. It had been growing into this for the last couple of years. He was almost nauseous from the fighting, bickering, barbs, and fiery exchanges.

He knew it was wrong.

He needed help.

> **Jesus Christ needs to give your marriage the same qualities you need as an individual.**

Pounding his fists on the steering wheel, he began to shout out loud: "God, you've got to do something! I can't go on with this any longer. I've got to have a change!"

He rarely ever shed a tear, but now Bill began to cry compulsively. His sobs turned to sighs of helplessness.

"Jesus, you're my Savior. Help me," he sighed.

Minutes passed. Slowly he composed himself, started the car, and drove away. As the streets passed by, God began to work in Bill, and he recalled those characteristics of Christlikeness I had shared. He turned each one over in his mind as if inspecting fresh fruit.

Suddenly, he began to see that the marks of Christlikeness were missing in his marriage.

He and Betty both, as individuals, knew those qualities in their lives. People even remarked on them, but they were not being produced in their marriage.

With a start, something occurred to him.

He and Betty had both been born again, but their marriage needed the same experience. Personally, apart, there were evidences of Christlikeness. Together in marriage, it was different.

He realized they needed Jesus Christ to give their marriage the same qualities they had prayed for as individuals.

Their marriage needed to be born again.

Quickly, he turned the car around and raced home.

"I need to talk to you," he said to Betty as he gently took her elbow and guided her upstairs. "Do you remember when Jesus came into your life?"

Of course she did.

Your marriage needs to be born again.

"Do you remember what Jesus began doing in your life when you received Him as your Savior?"

She nodded. "It was wonderful."

In the bedroom, they sat on the edge of the bed.

"When we married," he said intently, "we had a wedding ceremony, but that was it. We've never had family devotions. We've never really prayed together at home, only at church. We've never shared the Word together. Our boys have never seen us talk to God except over the meals."

She was weeping softly by now because of the tenderness in his voice and the truth she could feel in his words.

"Do you know what our marriage needs?" Bill asked her warmly and lovingly. "Our marriage needs to be born again."

As a mountain spring suddenly uncovered gushes fresh sparkling water, so they began to talk to each other, sharing their most intimate feelings and thoughts.

Bill had opened himself up to her for the first time in a decade and a half, exposing his thoughts, pouring out his heart, and asking her forgiveness for his many wrongs. Betty shared with him her longings, desires, and hurts. Together, they climbed over the walls of defensiveness they had built to protect themselves from vulnerability. They gave and received forgiveness.

It was in the early hours of the morning that they knelt by the bedside upon which they had sat and lain so long talking. There they called on Jesus to change their marriage.

Together, they asked God to make their marriage new. It was a new kind of reality for their marriage.

It became a new kind of life.

The next night Bill and Betty walked up the ramp of Angels Stadium in Anaheim, California, heading for their seats to enjoy the ballgame. They were like lovers who had just discovered each other. It was the awe of first love.

He stopped and turned to speak to her.

"Do you know, I think this is the greatest day of my life," he laughed. "I feel great. I feel absolutely free."

She kissed him, and they continued their climb.

"The End" had come and gone.

This was a brand-new marriage.

The ultimate happy ending became the ultimate blessed living.

Jesus was maximizing Bill's manhood.

CHAPTER 15

WHAT'S THE QUESTION?

Hiding a yawn, I listened to the couple differ in their perspectives of each other. My office was windowless and seemed airless as well. It was stuffy, and they seemed the same way.

I like people. I like to help them. But I was weary. The day had been one of those that had taken a great deal of time in counseling. I believe in counseling. I believe there is a bona fide ministry of counseling.

But I'm also convinced that the major reason for so much counseling in Christian lives today is that there is so little praying. When people spend time in the Word of God, meditating in it, praying over it, confessing it, the Word will become their counselor.

Suddenly, the woman sitting across from me jarred me fully awake with her statement.

"All I want him to do is to be a man. Just be a man."

I sat up straight and looked at her, then at him. It was a fair desire on her part. Her husband had exercised little leadership in the home. Because of that, his sons had lost all respect for him. The eldest was in the habit of mocking his father impudently. The other children were still under the mother's control, but only precariously. They constantly teased her with their escapades.

The woman was working to subsidize the income of the house because her husband would not look for a better paying position. He easily could have had one if he so desired. Because she was both disciplinarian and comforter for each of the children, as well as the co-breadwinner, she was wearied with her responsibilities.

Neither was there any spontaneity in their life—maritally, recreationally, or sexually. She wanted spice; he gave grits. She wanted something romantic and stimulating; he offered repetition and boredom.

Now, she had made her case. She had declared her desires.

"All I want him to do is to be a man. Just be a man."

I looked squarely at him. "You heard her," I said. "She wants a man. Can you give her one? She wants you."

He looked at me for a moment or two, eyeball-to-eyeball, then looked away. He gazed up at the ceiling for a long, long time.

The silence was like soil—growing awkwardness, flowering into tension.

The silence became so loud that it was almost deafening.

But I remembered to let him speak first. It was up to him to answer.

He had never been forced to decide before. His parents had always answered for him. His wife had learned over the years to do it for him as well. She was always compensating for him both in public and private, letting him hide behind her answers.

WHAT'S THE QUESTION?

But now, after two decades of schooling, marriage, children, and work, this man was going to have to answer for himself. His parents couldn't, and she wouldn't.

There are two great questions every man must face—not only face, but answer.

The first and most important in all of life is, *"What do you think about the Christ?"*

The second is, "Will you be a man?"

It was late. The office was stuffy, but the urge to doze was gone, replaced by the knife-edged sharpness in the room. Here was a man on the brink. His answer required manhood. Honesty, truthfulness, faith, humility, courage, love, grace—all the characteristics of manhood were now being called forth from the depths of his character. Here in the presence of his wife, his God, and his minister, he had to face the question, "Will you be a man?"

> Every man must answer the important question, "Will you be a man?"

His eyes swung down reluctantly from the ceiling and focused slowly on his wife's face. They sat not just eye-to-eye and face-to-face, but soul-to-soul.

He was obviously straining with the answer.

The words were only a faint whisper when they finally came, but it was like thunder in that room.

"I'll try."

Her face filled with happiness, tears sprang up, and she reached for him to embrace him. Holding him tight, squeezing and caressing him, it was as if some long lost lover had returned.

He would try.

Like the Prodigal, he had been in a far country. Now he had come to himself and was returning home. He would try.

What more could a woman ask? She could live with that, gladly. It had come from the depths of his soul, not lightly, but with the weightiness of his entire life. He had considered the question, confronted the issue, and declared his decision.

Manhood is not magic. It is a building process. No magic wand waved can produce it instantly. It doesn't strike like lightning. It is built, layer upon layer, line upon line, precept upon precept, decision upon decision.

The Bible says that everywhere Abraham went he *built* his altar and *pitched* his tents. Today, too many men are *building* their tents and *pitching* their altars. They spend too much time on the temporal and not enough on the eternal—too much time on building personality, while merely pitching character. It's a perversion of godly principles.

You can pitch personality, but you must build character.

One of my heroes of faith, W. T. Gaston, once told me something I have never forgotten and have quoted thousands of times: "When the charm wears off, you have nothing but character left."

It is the longing of every woman to have a man with character in the house. It is the need of every child to have a man at the helm. It is the crying need of every church to have real men at work in its ministry.

You can derive spirituality from women in the church, but you get strength from the men. It's the same in a home and in a nation. Churches, homes, and nations are only as strong as their men.

It is the command of our Father in heaven to be Christlike, and Christ Himself prayed to the Father to give His own Spirit to reproduce His life within us.

I said it before, I'm saying it again!

Manhood and Christlikeness are synonymous.

WHAT'S THE QUESTION?

Man has conquered the mountains, the oceans, and even outer space.

But the greatest achievement of all is when man conquers himself.

"He who rules his spirit [is better] *than he who takes a city"* (Proverbs 16:32).

Manhood and Christlikeness are synonymous.

Be a man!

Live a life of maximized manhood!

CHAPTER 16

ADULT BOYS

More than twenty years have gone by since writing that last chapter, and the world has changed dramatically in that span of time. Much of it in the increase of technology, change in physical geography, national boundaries, and in the culture of every country on the globe.

Today, instead of the absentee father being the curse of our day, it is "fatherlessness." The difference is that rather than being absent from the family, there is an absence of concern for the family. In a study by Columbia University, researchers discovered that children in single-parent homes led by a mother were better off than in homes with an unconcerned father. Fatherlessness is the curse of our day.

As never before, cultures have become the culprit in rape, drugs, divorce, disease, and other assorted ills. Many say the cause of all these evils is the breakdown of the family. The cause of the breakdown of the family is fatherlessness.

Sociologists say fatherlessness is caused by the immaturity of men. It is a pandemic problem in every nation on the planet Earth. Millions of parentless children will become problems, as prophesied in Isaiah 3:12: *"Children* [will become] *their oppressors."*

You are only young once, but you can live immature for a lifetime.

God commends childlikeness, but scorns childishness.

The whole purpose of the fivefold ministry gifts in the church is to enable men to mature—to grow up into the stature of the measure of being Christlike.

Since writing the first *Maximized Manhood,* I have carried the message that *"Manhood and Christlikeness are synonymous"* literally around the world. A member of the House of Lords in England exclaimed aloud in a meeting, "I have never heard such a truth before."

> **God commends childlikeness, but scorns childishness.**

When I teach concerning childishness, I make the statement that when a man acts like a child, it forces his wife to act like his mother. A more serious problem is that you can't make love to your mother. Reaction to that is almost always loud.

However, it is true. When his childishness causes problems in their intimate relationship, the man usually blames it on his wife—saying she is frigid. Doesn't understand him. The truth is, she understands him too well.

One of the more common features of childishness in a man today is addiction to pornography. Pornography, like all manner of sinfulness, promises to serve and please, but it only deceives and dominates. While promising intimacy, pornography provides it only with himself.

Pornography, a plague in modern society in every nation today, is idolatry. With it a man creates images in the mind to which the act of habitual masturbation is an act of worship, worshipping the idol or image created in the mind.

The "high places" of the mind are compared to the high places of idolatry that the nation of Israel created to take the place of worship to Jehovah God. We are to take *"every high thing that exalts itself against the knowledge of God"* (2 Corinthians 10:5), and cast it down, using the spiritual weapons of our warfare.

A childish man is an immature man.

Maturity doesn't come with age but begins with the acceptance of responsibility.

The first Adam in the Garden of Eden refused to accept responsibility for his actions, while the Last Adam, the Lord Jesus Christ, accepted responsibility for the actions of the entire world.

> **Maturity doesn't come with age, but with the acceptance of responsibility.**

Therein is the difference among men. At one end of the spectrum, some can't even accept responsibility for their own actions, and at the other end are men who not only accept responsibility for themselves but also for their families and for the world for which Christ died. The first are immature, childish men, but the last are mature, Christlike men of covenant.

Every man has the option to be a male, a man, or a covenant man.

Jesus asked, *"To what then shall I liken the men of this generation, and what are they like?"* (Luke 7:31).

He then answered His own question: *"They are like a group of children who complain to their friends, 'You don't like it if we play "wedding" and you don't like it if we play "funeral"'! For John the Baptist used to go without food and never took a drop of liquor all his life, and you said, 'He must be crazy!' But I eat my food and drink my wine, and you say, 'What a glutton Jesus is! And he drinks! And has the lowest sort of friends!' But I am sure you can always justify your inconsistencies"* (Luke 7:32–35 TLB).

A more contemporary saying is, "If I don't play by your rules, you will take your ball and go home!"

Grown men tell their wives, "It's my way or the highway." Childish!

A dictator in the Serbian conflict in Europe left the table where men had gathered to hammer out a peace treaty between races. As he left, he told them by both his language and his manner, "Because you don't want to play by my rules, I am not going to play." A supposedly mature and educated man acted like a child and caused the carnage to continue.

Some religious men are so steeped in their man-made traditions and ecclesiastical authority that they refuse to hear what Jesus says about them, like little children telling people, "If you don't live by my rules, you are not going to worship with me."

Jesus told such religious men that they rejected both Him and John the Baptist before Him, because neither He nor John accepted their man-made rules and regulations. These "religious" men were simply being childish, and in their pettiness, they insisted that others live by their philosophy, which was a rationalization created to justify their own failures.

When men live by someone else's philosophy that is a rationalization to justify their failures, men accept those failures.

Being able to overcome failure is a measure of mature manhood.

To live in and with it is not only stupid but immature.

We need to grow up!

"To learn, you must want to be taught," the proverb says. Availability is not the greatest need in business or ministry; teachability is. A person may be available, but if he cannot be taught, or is not willing to learn, it's no wonder he is available. It's hard to teach a man something that he thinks he already knows. No one wants someone who prefers ignorance over the humility it takes to learn.

"Religious" men are more concerned about their official status in their bureaucratic organizations than they are about their place in the kingdom of God.

Today's problem of immature men and pornography is fanned by the Internet. "Internet Porn" is so common today that it is almost accepted as a way of life. The standards of a previous generation have been obliterated by a cultural lifestyle and philosophy that views perversion and pornography as acceptable. Fifty-seven percent of the youth in America see nothing wrong with homosexuality or bisexuality.

> **The greatest need in business or ministry is teachability.**

Tolerance is the new politically correct word and way. College students must tolerate that which is biblically intolerable, and when they don't—by agreeing with God's Word instead—they are branded as bigots or worse and ostracized.

In his book *How God Saved the World*, Pastor Jim Garlow writes concerning the persecution of the church in the latter part of the second century: "Why were the emperors so set on killing believers? In addition to their refusal to claim Caesar as God, believers did not follow the traditional Roman gods and were considered intolerant of other religions."

But Christianity flourished in spite of the persecution. Tertullian, an early church leader, wrote, "Go on...torture, grind us to powder; our numbers increase in proportion as you mow us down. The blood of Christians is their harvest seed." Persecution failed to stop the growth of Christianity; instead, Christianity flourished.

Aggressively outspoken, Tertullian chose to use his witty and vigorous style to call Christians away from their lethargy and moral laxity to a rigorous and ascetic Christian faith. Tertullian applied his Christianity with great single-mindedness. He was deeply disturbed by the apathy of many believers in Carthage, a city with a population of three-quarters of a million people. One portion of his writing challenges Christians not only to live rigorous and disciplined lives, but also never to flee from persecution. Tertullian was drawn to the Christian faith in part because of the courage of the martyrs. It was he who first said that "the blood of the martyrs is the seed of the church," meaning that those who died for their faith brought others to faith.

Today, many young people are studying the martyrs, believing they may one day be one, while the "older, more mature, staid members" are sitting apathetically in their back pews. Many of the older generation now "tolerate" what they once shed from their lives in their youth.

Proverbs 14:14 says that *"the backslider gets bored with himself"* (TLB). As they attend church without the dynamic enthusiasm of loving Jesus, the Anointed One, our Messiah allows the so-called religious ones to find their excitement in places outside of the house of worship.

The people in the culture of our day, which is exchanging materialism for character—voting men into high office without concern for morality, ethics, or truthfulness; men who are deficient in character—are sowing to the wind but will reap the whirlwind. The world is being conditioned for acceptance of the Anti-christ, and we see the process throughout the world.

If ever there was a time and need for men to hold to the convictions of Scripture and take their stand for Christ, it is now.

The three Hebrew children taught us that we stand the tallest when everyone else is bowing.

Decision time is nearing!

Will you bow?

Or will you be standing tall for Jesus?

CHAPTER 17

IT'S THE HEART

Y ou sow to the future but reap from the past." My friend John Binkley said that referring to finances, but I could not help but think of it in reference to a couple who just announced they were filing for divorce.

Divorce has become so common in the culture, and immorality such an acceptable lifestyle, that it is having an influence on the culture of Christianity. A pastor announced his divorce to his congregation at the beginning of a Sunday service. Then when he introduced his new wife, the people stood and clapped joyously for them, after which they started the worship, and no one thought much about it—except that it was his second divorce and third wife.

When a pastor was found at an airport ready to fly from the U.S. to Europe for a two-week vacation, the airline personnel thought nothing of it. But when a parishioner from his church saw him there with a woman who was not his wife, the church thought a great deal of it.

Even after this trip with a woman he had met in a "chat room" was discovered, and his addiction to pornography was uncovered, a couple of men who served on the church board still wanted to retain him because he had caused the church to grow so much in the previous two years.

He had sown to the future, and now others were trying to keep him from reaping from his past.

Dr. Pearsall went to a medical doctor and stated that he was ill and needed treatment. For six months doctors told him he was not sick, until one of them finally agreed to do an MRI to prove it. The resonant imaging showed a tumor, found to be cancerous, in his pelvic area, exactly where Dr. Pearsall said he was ill. He came to believe his heart was telling him what the mind of men could not understand. Included in his findings is his belief that the heart comes before the mind in telling us about our bodies, and our lives.

Interesting!

The heart is formed before the brain in the womb.

It is the heart we should be listening to more than our minds, Dr. Pearsall says.

He gave a lecture on this subject, and a psychiatrist in the audience told of a patient of hers. An eight-year-old girl was the recipient of a heart transplant from a ten-year-old donor who was also a girl. The donor had been raped and murdered.

The mother of the eight-year-old became concerned for her daughter when she began to tell of dreams she was having. The mother took her to the psychiatrist who listened, and they both decided to report the dreams to the police.

Based on what the eight-year-old told the police, they arrested a neighbor of the ten-year-old who had been murdered. The eight-year-old had described in detail what the house was like where the murder occurred, what the room looked like, what the conversation was between her and the murderer, and it was so conclusive and correct that the neighbor was convicted of murder.

Consider, an eight-year-old recipient of the heart of a ten-year-old could recount in exact detail the murder that had occurred. The heart knew it. It was living. The body and brain of the donor were gone, but the heart lived because of the transplant, and the memory of the murder remained in the heart.

Scripture says, *"Keep your heart with all diligence, for out of it spring the issues of life"* (Proverbs 4:23). And, *"For as he thinks in his heart, so is he"* (Proverbs 23:7).

Jesus said, *"A good man out of the good treasure of his heart brings forth good things, and an evil man out of the evil treasure brings forth evil things"* (Matthew 12:35). It is from the heart, not from the mind, that good and evil come forth.

> **Good and evil come forth from the heart.**

It is why God made it possible for us through faith in Christ to be "born again," and to have a new heart, a heart that receives and contains the Spirit of God and brings forth the good things of Christ.

Jesus said, *"'You shall love the LORD your God with all your heart, with all your soul, with all your mind, and with all your strength.' This is the first commandment, and the second, like it, is this: 'You shall love your neighbor as yourself'"* (Matthew 22:37–39).

Notice, the heart comes first.

He did not say, "Love God with your soul, mind, and strength," but He put the heart first! Love must first be in the heart, both in love for God and for your wife. The heart comes first.

Divorce occurs when love grows cold or dies in the heart, or when a man says he loves a woman, but does it only with his mind and body.

"These people draw near with their mouths and honor Me with their lips, but have removed their hearts far from Me" (Isaiah 29:13). Jesus knows the hearts of men. He knows genuine love from the heart. First Samuel 16:7 says, *"The LORD looks at the heart."*

Religious men honor God with their souls, minds, and bodies, but their hearts aren't in it. They have never given their hearts to Him. It seems the heart gives it to the mind, but the mind can't love God righteously without the heart.

Loving God must emanate from, originate in, and be initiated by the heart. Dr. Pearsall's heart was telling him he was sick, but the minds of men could not understand knowledge that came from the heart. The heart knew what the mind could not understand. That's why we miss so much in life: we listen too much with our minds and miss what our hearts are telling us.

> **To love God you must love what God loves and hate what God hates.**

The heart that has become new in Christ is submitted to God's Word, lives by God's Word, and is empowered by obedience to God's Word.

The psalmist wrote, *"You who love the LORD, hate evil!"* (Psalm 97:10).

In Malachi 2:16, the prophet wrote, *"The LORD God of Israel says that He hates divorce."*

To love God you must love what God loves, and hate what God hates.

How can a man say he loves God if he loves what God hates?

Declension in morality follows the waning of love for God. The lesser the love for God, the lower the morality of an individual or a nation goes. Lower morality results in higher mortality, whether from physical or marital death.

As long as divorce is an option, you can never make a total commitment to the covenant of marriage. Marriage is a covenant, even as salvation is a covenant made with us through the shedding of Christ's blood on the cross. A covenant is more than a contract.

It's all a matter of the heart.

"For out of the heart proceed evil thoughts, murders, adulteries, fornications, thefts, false witness, blasphemies. These are the things which defile a man" (Matthew 15:19–20).

God knows our hearts, and knows our thoughts; the Devil doesn't. The Devil hears our words, sees our actions, watches what we love, and then does his damnable best to deceive, accuse, or tempt us according to what he knows about us.

God knows our hearts and made it possible for us to have new hearts, out of which come love, devotion, grace, mercy, compassion, and every good work.

The issue is always in the heart first.

In an arena with almost twenty thousand men, I concluded this teaching with the following, and I conclude this chapter with it. I mean no offense; I just want to be sure that you never forget this truth.

I told those men, "In case you don't understand what I have said, hear this: It's in the heart, stupid."

CHAPTER 18

TAKE IT TO THE CROSS

I t is difficult to live with change, but impossible to live without it. The only constant in maturity is change. How you handle change shows your level of maturity.

What you believe about God shows what you believe about yourself.

In the ensuing years since the first part of this book was written and published, it has been printed in more than forty languages. Almost two million copies have been printed, and it has been distributed through the Christian Men's Network to over two hundred nations of the world.

"Manhood and Christlikeness are synonymous" has become the central message, with the sentence itself now being a basic part of the Christian ministry lexicon.

At issue today is the message of the gospel story itself and its central truth. That truth concerns the cross, the symbol of Christianity. The symbol is not the manger or the empty tomb, but Calvary's cross. Jesus was born in a manger and was resurrected from the tomb, but redemption for man was accomplished on the cross.

The Bible is a book of history, poetry, proverbs, genealogies, law, prophecy, doctrine, and biography. The cross is the centerline of the Bible. In the Old Testament are the Pentateuch, history, poetry, and prophecy, and in the New Testament are the Gospels, history, Epistles, and Revelation.

The cross is the culminating place of worship. First an altar, then the tabernacle, the temple, and finally Calvary.

The cross is the centerline of the Bible, the place of worship, the place of exchange.

The cross is the place of exchange. When you go to the cross, you leave different from the way you came.

"Take it to the cross" is the title and banner under which eternal change takes place in our lives. We take:

Guilt—and leave with acquittal
Repentance—and leave with faith
Sorrow—and leave with joy
Sin—and leave with righteousness
Stupidity—and leave with wisdom
Ignorance—and leave with eternal knowledge
Disease—and leave with healing
Rejection—and leave with acceptance
Impotence—and leave with power

You get the idea. The cross takes an old life and makes it become a new creation in Christ Jesus. *Take it to the cross!*

God's love is connected to the cross. The cross is God's display of love for the world. To tell of God's love without telling of the cross is an egregious error.

The cross is where God's wrath against sin was appeased by Christ's sacrifice, so that God could be just in forgiving guilty man.

None of us can live according to the law, because we are lawbreakers by nature. We are all guilty of breaking the law. Consider the commandments God gave. If you break one, it's as if you have broken them all. None of us has ever been able to keep them all, and most of us have broken all of them—in one way or another. Therefore, we need someone to forgive us of our lawbreaking.

The reason God gave the law was to use it as a schoolmaster to teach us that we are lawbreakers, and thus sinners. If sinners, then we are in need of some means to take away our sin and make us righteous in the sight of God.

The law shows us that we are sin-sick by nature and in need of a cure.

If the law is not fully understood, the sinner won't appreciate the grace of God that emanates from the cross. To minister grace without the knowledge of the law is like giving a man medicine when he doesn't know he is sick. Men fail to appreciate a cure if they don't know they are sick.

The law shows us that we are sin-sick by nature. We are in need of a cure. The cure is the free gift of salvation in Christ Jesus, but if we don't admit we are sick, the cure means nothing to us.

The Devil's temptation in the Garden of Eden was to assure Adam and Eve that if they took of the tree they would be as God. Humanism! Hasn't changed from then until now. The Devil's lie is to make us think we are good enough for God by our own efforts. Liar!

Peter and the disciples were with Jesus when He asked them, *"Who do men say that I, the Son of Man, am?"* (Matthew 16:13). Peter answered as to what "they" said, and "they" were all wrong. "They" usually are.

Then Jesus asked, *"But who do **you** say that I am?"* (verse 15, emphasis added). Peter answered, *"You are the Christ, the Son of the living God"* (verse 16). Jesus commended him for the answer, declaring that man had not taught him that, but that he had spoken it by revelation from the Father in heaven (verse 17).

Later, Jesus *"began to show to His disciples that He must go to Jerusalem, and suffer many things from the elders and chief priests and scribes, and be killed, and be raised the third day"* (verse 21).

Peter took Jesus aside and began to reprove and charge Him for talking like that. *"Far be it from You, Lord; this shall not happen to You!"* (verse 22).

> **The Devil will tempt you according to your worth in the kingdom of God.**

Jesus *"turned and said to Peter, 'Get behind Me, Satan!'"* (verse 23). In other words, Jesus told Peter that he was sounding just like the Devil. Peter was not speaking by revelation as he had before, but like a man who was not partaking of the nature and quality of God.

Why did Jesus tell Peter he was sounding like the Devil?

Because one of the Devil's temptations was to offer Jesus all the kingdoms of this world, if He would bow down and worship the Devil (Matthew 4:8–9). Satan was tempting Jesus according to His worth in the kingdom of God. So also, the Devil will tempt you according to your worth in the kingdom of God. The more worth you are to God's kingdom, the more the Devil will offer you to serve him.

The Devil was attempting to keep Jesus from going to the cross.

However, Jesus knew: "No cross, no crown!" The only way to redeem sinful man was by His sacrificial death upon the cross. Only through that redemptive offering could you and I be forgiven of our sins and enter into a covenant relationship with God through Jesus Christ. The covenant was to be a blood covenant through the blood shed upon the cross.

That same blood is now before the mercy seat in heaven, and on the basis of that offering we have God's mercy and grace to forgive us and reconcile us to Himself. No greater sacrifice can be made than that which Christ made at the cross.

Peter sounded like the Devil by trying to keep Jesus from going to the cross. To omit the cross is to make Christianity just like any other religion on the face of the earth. It is the Devil's purpose to keep men like you and me from "taking it to the cross."

We cannot bear Christ's cross; He will not bear ours. We must take up our crosses and follow.

The cross is where Jesus triumphed over principalities and powers. It is the place where Satan's power is broken. At the cross we are crucified to the world, and the world is crucified to us.

After rebuking Peter, Jesus continued to tell His disciples, *"If anyone desires to come after Me, let him deny himself, and take up his cross, and follow Me"* (Matthew 16:24). Notice, He did not say for us to take up *His* cross and follow Him, but for us to take up *our* cross and follow Him.

We cannot bear Christ's cross; He will not bear ours. We must take up our cross and follow. What is our cross? What is His cross?

Our Lord took up His cross in the Garden of Gethsemane, but was nailed to the cross on Calvary. As He prayed in the Garden, with such intensity that blood, rather than sweat, burst through His pores, He asked the Father if it was possible to keep Him from going to the cross. He was going to be made sin for us, take upon Himself God's wrath against sin, taste our death, and it was reprehensible to His sinless person.

"If it is possible, let this cup pass from Me; nevertheless, not as I will, but as You will" was Jesus' prayer in Matthew 26:39. When He submitted to the will of the Father, and admitted His willingness to die so that we might have life, He took up his cross.

> **Jesus' cross was to do the will of God at the expense of Himself.**

His cross was the willingness to do the will of God, even at the expense of Himself.

He told you and me to take up our crosses and follow Him to be His disciples. What is our cross? The same as His!

Our cross is the willingness to do the will of God, even at the expense of ourselves.

Even as Christ died on the cross, we must die to ourselves so that the will of God can be done in our lives.

"Take it to the cross!"

Where is the cross in the life of the man who walks out of his house and marriage yelling, "I just want to live"? He is willing to let the marriage die and live himself, rather than ensuring that his marriage lives and he dies to himself.

Think about it.

CHAPTER 19

THAT'S MY DAD!

Your talent can take you where your character can't sustain you. This is true of athletes and CEOs as well as preachers.

The legacy of a father is the character he instills in his son and daughter. Three of the greatest words any man can hear are, "That's my dad!"

Government is powerless to make people stay married, cause parents to love their children, make parents raise their children properly, or force parents to keep their promises to their children. One of the major reasons for writing against divorce as I do came from a child of divorce who said, "My childhood stopped when my parents divorced."

In her book about stepfamilies, Joann Webster writes, "People shouldn't think twice about getting a divorce—they should think about it fifty thousand times and still not do it."

Judith Wallerstein writes in her book *The Unexpected Legacy of Divorce*, a twenty-five-year case study, "Children of divorce never recover from it." She shows the results of divorce in the children's lives and how it affects them as adults.

Society, which begins in the church, must affirm traditional marriage as vital, teach parents to love and care for their children, strengthen families to strengthen the community, and teach children the importance of relationships.

Home is the school of first instruction. Our children are the leading indicator of the future of our nation.

A man's life is summed up in, or founded on, three things: stewardship, relationships, and leadership. All three are vitally important with children.

> **A man's life is founded on three things: stewardship, relationships, and leadership.**

To be a father is to be the procreator of a human life that is formed and fashioned in the image and likeness of God. That is a sacred matter. A child is to be the product of love—not lust. Too often when it is just lust, the life given is not regarded as sacred, and abortion is the result.

As a father you are responsible for the child you have conceived.

You are responsible for the child you made the mother abort.

You are responsible for the child that you abandoned, who is now on drugs, in jail, or involved in prostitution.

You are responsible for the fatherless children made that way by your irresponsibility.

You sit here reading this book, and somewhere there is a fatherless child on the streets whom you put there, and you don't give a @#$%*! And you are more concerned about the word I just intended than the child about whom I am talking.

Sons and daughters are born; fathers are made.

Any male can conceive a child, but only a man can father a child.

No man has the right to impregnate a woman and get her with child unless he is willing to father the child that is born. No man!

We, as men, are called to raise G–rated children in an X–rated world.

Our responsibility is to raise trustworthy children who respect and admire their father.

God's admonition to us is not to provoke them to wrath, but to *"bring them up in the training and admonition of the Lord"* (Ephesians 6:4). To do that takes time. Quality time. There is no substitute for time. To give time is to give yourself, and that is what it takes.

I was privileged to be the speaker at a Promise Keepers meeting at the Los Angeles Coliseum, where 78,462 men were in attendance. I said something and the whole crowd let out a concerted groan. All I said was, "A practicing atheist does not stand on a street corner and shake his fist at heaven shouting that he doesn't believe in God. He just lives as if there is no God. Most of you go to church on Sunday, then come home and do nothing spiritual during the week—like reading the Bible or praying—and to all intents you are a professing Christian on Sunday and a practicing atheist during the week." GROAN!

> **Any male can conceive a child, but only a man can father a child.**

The apostle Paul gave the premise for a good father when he said, *"Imitate me, just as I also imitate Christ"* (1 Corinthians 11:1).

The scriptural account of Moses en route to taking up the mantle of leadership of Israel says that he became ill to the point of death. His wife, Zipporah, circumcised their eldest son, and Moses became well, then continued on his journey. Strange insertion in just a couple of verses. Why?

Because our Lord said, *"If you were Abraham's children, you would do the works of Abraham"* (John 8:39). Abraham is the father of God's family of faith on earth. All believers in Christ realize they are descendants by faith through faithful Abraham. God's commendation of him was simple, *"I have known him, in order that he may command his children and his household after him"* (Genesis 18:19).

What were the works of Abraham that he passed on to his descendants? First, he obtained righteousness by faith; second, he tithed; third, he rescued Lot; fourth, he commanded his family after him. God proved and qualified Abraham to be the leader of His heavenly family on earth through leading his earthly family. That is why Paul wrote to Timothy and told him that a minister must first prove himself a leader of his own family before he can lead the family of God in church.

Abraham was responsible to circumcise his son, give him an inheritance, teach him a trade, and find him a wife.

It was Moses' responsibility to circumcise his son, and he failed to do it. Why? I don't know. From practical experience I could imagine him being so busy with the call of God on his life that he left it up to his wife to care for the family. His wife, Zipporah, did not have the same heritage, upbringing, or understanding of Jehovah and Abraham that he had; thus, when she was forced to do it, she told him off. His sin of neglecting this most important aspect of life—fathering—could have resulted from his being unequally yoked with a Midianite, who was too indulgent of her child, and Moses was too indulgent of her.

God taught Moses a lesson before he assumed the role of captain of the Lord's people. Moses was without excuse.

God taught him in a most severe way that no man is an exception to God's laws!

God made it plain, in no uncertain terms, that no man is exempt from God's ways! No man can absent himself from God's Word.

Eli was a priest in Israel. He studied the writings. He knew his responsibility, yet his sons became "sons of Belial." Devilish, profane, selfish, base, and worthless, they made the people of Israel sin by their wickedness. Eli heard what his sons did and reproved them. He failed, however, to remove them from leadership in Israel. In failing to so, God told Eli he was honoring his sons above Him.

God judged Eli harshly, but justly. He cut off his posterity.

What happened to this poor old man that he would suffer such a fate at the end of his long career in the service of God?

He might have made his ministry, which was his career, his idol. Perhaps, he paid more attention to it than he did to the Lord. So many men do that to this day. It is not an uncommon practice, but it is unscriptural. For all intents and purposes, he made his sons fatherless. They were not streetwise, but churchwise, by definition being religious, profane, manipulative, doing things only to impress, deceptive, and hard-hearted. Not uncommon but unspiritual.

Consider the works of a real father, a real son of Abraham, a genuine son of God.

First, circumcise your son. The New Testament equivalent would be to make sure your children are genuine Christians, born of God's Spirit. God gave to the father the responsibility to see that his children know the Lord. God holds the man responsible. Too often, the man leaves the spiritual influence to his wife. By forfeiture she becomes responsible. Men suffer from this and do not even know it. By refusing to accept the God-given responsibility to be the spiritual leader of the family, he comes under the judgment of God and wonders why he is not blessed of God. Very obvious!

Second, give him an inheritance. Abraham gave his sons a great inheritance in faith and finances. It was their responsibility to steward the gifts and see them increase, not decrease or decline. If God did not want sons to inherit the father's ministry, he would not be known as the God of Abraham, Isaac, and Jacob. However, they had to re-dig the wells of Abraham their father. Sons can inherit ministries, but they cannot inherit the anointing. They must get that for themselves from God alone. In business it is the same. Until the son proves himself, he cannot assume leadership, nor will his leadership be accepted.

Make sure your children are born of God's Spirit.

Third, teach him a trade. In many countries and in many ways, an apprenticeship is still common. In some countries such as the United States, it is not as common. But the father can teach his son a work ethic, the value of money, and lessons that will prepare him for life.

Fourth, find him a wife. In some countries arranged marriages are still made. In Abraham's day they did not marry the one they loved, but they did love the one they married. In the United States today too often we marry the one we love, then do not love the one we marry.

A father might not arrange a marriage today, but he can teach his children the sacredness of the marriage covenant and its value in the sight of God, and the glory of virginity. Virginity is the one gift God gives a man and woman that they can give one time to one person in one lifetime. That is why it is so special and sacred. As a single person, God has given you something so special, so meaningful, so precious, so sacred, that he has given you that one gift to give one time to one person in one lifetime.

Being a good father is the noblest calling on earth.

Being a stepfather can require more grace and wisdom than being a natural father, because a stepfather must earn the right of authority, whereas the natural father has it birthed into the family.

The principle Jesus gave is vital for stepfathers and the children he has gained by marriage. *"If you have not been faithful in what is another man's, who will give you what is your own?"* (Luke 16:12).

In one of our Phoenix events a man stood to his feet and said, "I could never understand why I was having problems with my two stepchildren that I did not have with my own two. When I heard that, it hit me that I have not been as faithful to my stepchildren as I have to my own, so beginning tomorrow, there will be no difference between any of our children." Every man there stood and cheered.

Why is the man so important?

The first five books of the Bible are simply the stories of seven men.

God's story is revealed through men.

God reveals himself as our Father.

We can reveal ourselves to those we have birthed as their father. Because the priest in the Old Testament was the intercessor between God and man, the mediator, the one who ministered God's grace to the people in his care, and were called "father," so the father in the home acts as "priest" for the family.

That's why no man has the right to talk to his children about God until he has talked to God about his children.

Prophet, priest, king, dad, father—be a man, a real man—Christlike in all you do in and with your family. They need it, society needs it, and the kingdom of God needs it.

CHAPTER 20

BURN OUT; DON'T FADE OUT

God loves you the way you are, but loves you too much to leave you the way you are. People hear what you say, but learn from what you are. What you are is shown by what you do. Actions speak louder than words.

The difference between men who fail and those who succeed, more often than not, is their ability to handle pressure. Proverbs, in *The Living Bible,* says, *"You are a poor specimen if you can't stand the pressure of adversity"* (Proverbs 24:10).

When I wrote the first part of this book, the quickening power of God was on the writing, and I felt that I could not improve on what was written, no matter the time in which it was written. I realize the anointing abides, and around the world men have had their lives changed from reading the truth.

In Zimbabwe, at a conference where I was speaking, a God-fearing man challenged me. Reverend Perkins had been a missionary for over thirty years in Zambia and was revered and loved. He had been beaten and left for dead by the side of a road, wrapped with barbed wire, and left to die. He not only lived, but lived long enough to see those who had mistreated him brought to Christ. That was the justice he desired.

My first sight of him was when he was introduced to speak at the conference, and walked to the podium, slowly but emphatically. He stood looking at the audience for several minutes. Then he spied me on the front row. What happened then startled all of us and amazed me.

"Where were you when I needed you?" he bellowed at me. "I have spent my lifetime ministering to women and children, and only now have read your book *Maximized Manhood*. If I had spent my life majoring in men I could have saved my nation. You need to be in the bush where you're needed."

My heart pounded, my face flushed, and I shook in my seat from the force of his words. Never had I been addressed like that before, nor have I since. I have never forgotten the sight of him nor the power of his words.

Though I never went to the bush, I have never stopped ministering to men or ceased writing about and addressing their needs. Partners of this ministry have gone, and we have sent truckloads of books.

After almost fifty years of ministry and fifty-four years of marriage, I am still traveling, writing, teaching, and preaching. Living for Christ is the single greatest adventure on earth. There is nothing like it.

I was having a bite to eat recently with a friend who looked at me and said, "I give you the right to speak into my life. Anything you see that needs to be changed, tell me. Or if I am doing something wrong, please let me know. Some ministers do it without my permission, but I give you the right because I know you will tell me the truth."

I paused for a long time and then gave him my final answer.

"Faded glory!"

He stared at me to understand the meaning of my answer and then inquired, "What do you mean?"

"Don't live in faded glory," I said. "Nancy was telling me the other day that we needed new wallpaper in our kitchen, new paint in the bedroom, and new carpeting in some areas. When we moved in, she had it all remodeled

Don't live in faded glory.

and redone, and it looked beautiful. But now the glory of that day years ago is faded, and it needs replacement and redoing again. She can't stand to live in faded glory."

"I don't understand," he said.

"Nancy and I were talking about the early days of our lives, when we were both converted. How we would not miss a church service, prayer meeting, or witnessing on the streets. How the glory of God filled our hearts, and the fire of God burned so brightly on the altars of our hearts! Then she said again something we have said over the years.

"Edwin, I was born in the fire and can't stand to live in the smoke."

"What has that to do with me?" my friend asked.

"When you started out over twenty years ago, the glory of God filled everything you did. You learned how to work, worship, lead men, witness, teach, sell—whatever a man must do—and now you are a success, but you are still doing the same thing the same way.

"You have added some things, but basically it has grown old through the years. You need to take another look at it all so that you don't live with faded glory. You live a contemporary life of faith, enjoy prosperity, but when people look at what you have, they see things worn and old. You believe one thing but let them look at another and put them in a mental bind.

"A marriage can be in the same condition. The man says it is great, and the wife says in is moribund. Maybe not quite dead, but mediocre at best. Things have become lukewarm over the years, tepid, at best, and the glory of the honeymoon has long gone out of it. The wonder, awe, passion, and love have waxed cold, or old, and it is not the same. She tries to tell him, but he won't listen, until—like God's taste toward lukewarmness—it is spewed out of the mouth.

"Or it can happen in a business, where sameness was an aim and purpose when it first began but is now the reason for boredom, half-heartedness, and mediocrity. You push hard to increase the business, but can't get beyond your level of maintenance into fresh creativity.

"I was ministering for a pastor in Chicago when the Holy Spirit took over in one of those electric 'God moments' while I was speaking. Looking at his congregation, I told them that some of them were finding fault with the pastor, complaining about not having access to him or being unable to have the same relationship with him that they had enjoyed years ago. The problem is that he had grown to new levels, but they never had. They complained about faded glory, when they were the ones who refused to pay the price to grow as he had. That's faded glory.

"It's the same in America. Our country was started in the glory of a thirst, desire, and passion to have and live in religious freedom, to escape the evil punishment of loving God's printed page. The glory of the nation's founding is recorded over and over again, and there are those in the country who have been welcomed with open arms. Come enjoy life, liberty, and the pursuit of happiness.

"Only they brought their own gods with them and refused to acknowledge the God of all grace, and His Son, the Lord Jesus Christ, who paid the price for us to have freedom not only from the bondage of sin and Satan, but also from authorities who rejected Him. As a result, the glory of America is fading.

"Indifference to the history that gave us such glory, anguish over the command to have no other gods before Him, and hatred toward those who adhere to the principles and convictions in God's Word are but some of the symptoms of faded glory in this great God-given land.

"Rather than the flag being the emblem of the bloodstains of those who died for it, and stars representing its magnificent structure—being something worthy of awe and even rapture as it waves grand and high—it is met with a yawn, a nonchalance, and those who hate it have the legal rights to burn it.

"Men resting on the old, faded glory. Marriage partners who began with glory, blessing, wonder, and gratitude now accept divorce as casually as going to the theater. Patriotism lost to a whole new generation who never had to pay a price for the country in which they live. Churches and parishioners who began in the glory of God now live in the afterglow of what once was, talking about the past as if it were the present. Talking about what was, but now isn't.

"Faded glory. Believers who gave offerings sacrificially, and as generously as they gave themselves to God, now resent the blessings of giving. They cynically charge the ministry with self-serving purposes, but do not realize that their refusal to give is because they have lost the vision of the lost."

As we left the restaurant, he said he would never forget those words.

I hope you will not either.

In the Old Testament, after Solomon prayed, the glory of God filled the temple. Time went by and the temple was still there, but the gold was gone and brass had been put in its place—a sign of faded glory—what was, but now isn't.

Peter wanted to build three tabernacles and stay in the glory of Jesus on the Mount of Transfiguration. The Lord said, "No." His glory could not be put in a box, but in a tabernacle *"made without hands"* (Mark 14:58).

The fleshly nature of man will always want to relax, take it easy, find a resting place, and not be subject to the disciplines of the spirit that hunger and thirst for God, seek the daily application of Bible study and prayer, and want to be part of what God is doing on the earth in this hour!

Nancy said it best, "Edwin, let's not just fade away, but let's burn out for Jesus."

General MacArthur, after retiring, said, "Old soldiers never die; they just fade away."

That is the way of the flesh, the world, the earth, and man, but not God!

I want to be fired up for God until I die.

Why miss the best part of your life, which is *today*? Yesterday did not have the good old days; today is the best day of our lives!

God's glory never fades; people do.

His glory is the same yesterday, today, and forever.

We have been *"[born anew] into an inheritance which is beyond the reach of change and decay [imperishable], unsullied and unfading, reserved in heaven for you"* (1 Peter 1:4 AMP).

Enjoy it, because it is going to last for an eternity.

MAJORING IN MEN

Ben Kinchlow and I were sitting in the Polo Lounge Room of the Beverly Hills Hotel having breakfast. It is the kind of place you get to only once. Ben had ordered steak and eggs—my treat.

Ben is a friend, a brother, and a real man.

While sitting there in the elegant surroundings, enjoying the benefits of waiters who never let your coffee get cold or your water glass empty, we were talking about the tremendous things God had done for our families.

There was a pause in the conversation. We both sat there in easy, brotherly comfort, enjoying each other's company, when suddenly Ben threw his napkin over his face and just sat there for a moment.

"What happened?" I solicitously inquired, sotto voce.

He looked at me with a seriousness that I have never forgotten.

"You know," he began slowly, "there was a time in my life when I did not have anything. Nothing. I wanted something, man, and I wanted it badly. Do you realize there was a time when I would have sold my wife into prostitution, taught my kids to steal, done anything just to sit in a place like this, seeing famous people and being somebody? I thought that kind of power and prestige were the answers for me.

"Man, you don't know what I went through. All the hell, all the suffering, all the pain. My life was nothing. I was nothing.

"And to think—to have it all—all I had to do was give my life to Jesus Christ."

Ben was enjoying some of his Canaan Land life.

It certainly wasn't just this treat to a fancy breakfast; it was how his whole life—his family, occupation, self-image—had changed completely.

And Ben isn't alone.

Men, the Canaan Land life is for all of us, if we can only understand the way to get there. My desire to help in pointing the way has been intense.

At the outset of this book, I described that eventful men's retreat in Oregon. What happened there fanned the ember in my heart into a roaring flame. I wanted to reach out to men throughout the nation and even beyond.

A few months later, in May of 1980, I was speaking at a national conference in Pittsburgh, when, in the midst of my message, I stopped, looked at the audience, and then spontaneously blurted, "Pray for me, that God will release me into a national ministry to men."

Their response was as if an electric current had moved through the room. They immediately began to clap their hands, some jumped to their feet, and everywhere people began to pray. Their hearts had confirmed that the ministry was desperately needed.

In November of that year, my wife, Nancy, and I had a gathering in a home in Huntington Beach of friends and others who believed God was calling me to a ministry for men. It was an intercessory prayer meeting, and as they prayed, one vein began to pulsate in their prayers—that God would enable me to minister to 10,000 men during the forthcoming year of 1981. As they prayed, it became apparent that it was the Holy Spirit speaking, and I received the message as a God-given goal.

During the first three months of 1981, my life was so busy it was incredible. Serving two television networks, being chancellor of a school of ministry and senior minister of a parish, plus conducting men's rallies was more than too much for me. But by God's grace, I was doing it all, and things seemed to be thriving.

Nancy and I planned a meeting for all those who shared in our ministry later that year, at the Marriot Hotel in Newport Beach. We wanted to let them know what had been happening and what our future plans were.

George Otis said he had a "word" for us, and he flew in from Chicago on his way to Israel. I should have known by that strange route that something important was going to happen. George Otis began to speak, and it seemed as if my life opened before my eyes. It had been over thirty years—since the night God anointed me to preach the Gospel—that I had felt anything like what was happening to me at that moment. It was as if I were being called to the ministry all over again.

One phrase George spoke pierced my heart. *"This ministry is running late."*

Those words were like a scalpel performing open-heart surgery within me.

Within twenty-four hours, I had written letters of resignation for every position I held, releasing myself from all of my other commitments. It was time to major in men.

Sunday morning, Nancy and I went to the church where I was still the senior pastor. When it came my time to speak, I looked at the congregation quietly for a moment, then I began:

"This may be one of the most unique services you will ever be in because, when I leave, I will not be back. This is my final service. God has said I'm 'running late,' and I need to catch up."

Sure enough, after the benediction, Nancy and I left. We love those brothers and sisters, but we had to answer God's directive.

Tough. Decisive. Courageous.

There is a difference between reading the Bible and living it—as much difference as there is between heaven and hell, Egypt and Canaan.

The following Monday, I took my typewriter into my den and began to "catch up."

We heard from many during that week—that we should not be starting a ministry now, the economy was bad, we were too old, it could never be done, we should think about retirement, and a welter of other negative comments. But we were able to brush them aside, because the call from God was so clear; we knew what had to be done. And we are doing it. Or, should I say, God is doing it.

In Virginia Beach, Ben Kinchlow was impressed to pray for us that we would personally minister to 100,000 men in 1982. That would be a tenfold increase from the year before.

By July, two other people were helping us, and we moved into my garage to work. Nothing like dictating in the front seat of a car or answering the phone sitting on the washer/dryer. From there we grew to rented office space. Then, years later we moved to our International Communications Center centrally located just outside Dallas, Texas.

But after two months, we grew even more, and in September, we had to move to offices in town at Corona del Mar. We have added three times since then to both office space and personnel.

Twenty-one years have passed since the first part of this book was written. People have changed. Our statement, *"Manhood and Christlikeness are synonymous,"* has become part of the Christian lexicon in a large part of the body of Christ. The anachronistic "one-dollar tip" seems almost insulting, yet it made all the difference back then. But the truth has lived on.

Four years after the book came out, I was challenged by a pastor who wanted to know what "my follow-up" program was to my men's events.

My reply was always, "The pastor is."

Then one day as I was teaching a group of pastors, one of them interrupted me, saying forcefully, "This is the most intimidating meeting I have ever been in." I was shocked, immediately wondered what I had said, and started to apologize for whatever it was. Then he interrupted me again.

"No! Don't apologize. I can run the church, preach the sermons, develop the programs, but I don't know if I can disciple a man!"

As I left that day I realized he had just told me something, which because of my pastoral experience, I had not understood until that moment.

The average pastor did everything except disciple men, yet it was the one thing Jesus gave a commandment to do: "Go and make disciples."

The following year I launched the Christian Men's Network to send the message on videocassette to places to which I could never go in person. Those videos have gone literally around the world, to 210 nations at the time of this printing.

Maximized Manhood has been translated into more than forty languages, with approximately two million copies in print. Ten more books have been written with another million in print. *Maximized Manhood* is the basic teaching tool still, and along with other books, it forms a "Majoring in Men Curriculum" that is now being taught by pastors and men in churches and groups worldwide.

Ben Kinchlow, who wrote the introduction, has left *The 700 Club* and is traveling and ministering around the world. He is still a close friend, and we see each other as often as possible.

My son, Paul, after having his own television production company, where among other things he developed and produced the "Farm Aid" event for singer Willie Nelson, came and ministered with me for years. Now, Paul has announced he will become a pastor. Nancy announced she "would be Charter Member Number One." And, of course, in her eyes, he is the greatest preacher and minister in the world; God only knows where I come in on her scale of approval.

Joann, who was in Bible school when she gave me the word that "sex sins will be the problem of the church in the eighties," went as a missionary to Japan, then operated the Network ministry with me, edited my new books with me, and is now a full-fledged writer and author on her own. After she married Richard, they gained custody of his two children as budding teenagers, and with one of them, she has written a best-selling book about stepfamilies. Get it.

My daughter Lois spent thirteen years as a Deputy District Attorney in California, then moved to Texas to be near the family, and launched a conservative newspaper column. Today she is beginning a new career as an author in her own right.

My wife, Nancy, is still the *"Loveliest Lady in the Land,"* and has never lost her ability to help me. Once she told me, "Why don't you go back and read your book again." Ouch! But, oh, so funny!

We have been married over fifty years. People ask me if I have been married to the same woman for that many years. My answer is always, "NO! She is lovelier, more gracious, loyal, godly, purer than she ever was. She is the greatest mother, minister's wife, lover, and the finest Christian I have ever met in my life."

The pastor who had the problem with the music minister has long since retired, and the music minister now leads worship for a "metropolitan" congregation.

The minister who was coordinator for our initial event in Oregon later moved to northern California and had an outstanding ministry.

Owen Carr has gone to be with the Lord.

Earl Book went on to a career as a superintendent in his denomination, and I lost track of him.

Pat Robertson has continued with the Christian Broadcasting Company to reach out around the world in massive crusades through television, and the results count hundreds of thousands of men and women who have come to the knowledge of Christ as Savior and Lord. He gave us our first $10,000 gift to start the Network, and we still have a warm friendship.

I wrote about a man who was in business and knocked on my door. That introduction became a friendship when he became a Christian and attended the church I pastored. Today he is still in the real estate business, still married to the same wonderful woman, and serves on our Board of Directors in the Network.

"Steve and Gail," who recovered from his adultery, are still together today. I just spent time with them a month ago. He's just as funny and she's just as vivacious as they ever were. Their daughter who once stood at death's door is a grown woman, serving God today.

Reverend LaFayette Scales came into my life in the late '80s, ministered with me in South Africa during the years of apartheid, and although he is black, he left a lasting impression on Africa and Africa made an impression on him. He has since become one of the foremost ministers to men in America and also serves on our Network Board of Directors. Ironically, he was in the audience in Pittsburgh when I asked for those attending to agree in prayer with me to launch this ministry. He agreed, and the rest is history.

So many in the book have passed through my life and gone on. Though I didn't often use real names, they were real people, and I wrote about them as a lesson for all of us. To them, wherever they may be, whether they know I wrote about them or not, I thank them for their input into my life—and yours.

Men who have been ministered to and nurtured through the ministry over the years are now doing the teaching themselves; and the truths that I taught, they have expanded, improved, and given away better than they received them originally.

As I spoke to a group of athletes in Larry Kerrychuk's conference in Phoenix, a young football coach was in attendance. After hearing the message, "Your Word Is Your Bond," he was so moved that he went home to tell the men he was meeting with that they should name their group, "Promise Keepers."

The Lord is moving on men's hearts as only He can, and I am so grateful to Him to be a part of it.

EPILOGUE: MAJORING IN MEN

Nancy is the one who recognized why some men do not enter Canaan. She said one night, "The Israelites sent spies into the land, and they believed their negative report instead of the promises of God. I believe it was because of their poor self-image of unworthiness and inferiority. They could not believe God would give them all He had promised.

"That's the way it is with us, too. We have to die to that old self-image that the world, the Devil, and sin has stamped on our hearts and minds. That is why men have to have the new image of Jesus Christ stamped on them instead, so they can go into Canaan Land.

"Make sure they understand that," she said intensely.

That's exactly what I'm doing.

Ben Kinchlow sat in the Polo Lounge Room with a brand-new image of himself—one that Jesus Christ gave him because Ben was letting the Holy Spirit renew the spirit of his mind with the authority of God's Word, and it made a new man out of him.

I've watched men from every walk of life come to the meetings as one kind of man and leave as another. God's commands produce the same result in every man whoever or wherever he may be.

God can do the same for you.

Repent of those sins; turn from them—now!

If you have never asked Jesus to forgive you of your sins, now is the time, and this is the place. If you believe in your heart that Jesus is Lord, but have never confessed Him with your mouth, this is the time to do it.

Romans 10:10 says that it is with the heart that man believes and is made *righteous,* and with the tongue he confesses and is given salvation.

So say these words, aloud, right where you are:

"Right now, without any shame or embarrassment; without any hesitation; in front of everybody I know—family, friends, neighbors—I confess that Jesus Christ is my personal Savior.

"I believe that when I asked Him to, Jesus forgave me of all my sins and sent His Spirit into my heart.

"Let the angels rejoice at my words right now because I declare on earth that Jesus Christ is Lord, and I declare it to the glory of God the Father.

"Let the Devil tremble at my words! I publicly confess that Jesus Christ is the Son of God, that He came from heaven to earth, was born of a virgin, and lived a sinless life. He went about doing good and healing everybody oppressed by the Devil. He went to the cross and died for the sins of the world, after which they laid Him in a grave.

"But He rose from the dead! And at this very moment, as I pray, He sits at the right hand of the Father in heaven.

"Right now, because of His Spirit in me, I have His victory over the grave, death, hell, the world, the flesh, the Devil, and I praise Him for it.

"Right now, Lord, I ask You to bring miraculous changes into my entire life, believing that You will answer me. I praise You for it now!"

Friend, in this confession and prayer, you have just obeyed God. Believe that God will answer your prayer and bring mighty changes into your mind, heart, soul, body, and entire life.

I am believing God's promises for you, right now.

Don't let someone else create your world for you. For when they do, they will always make it too small.

God is a big God, and He has big plans for you!

EPILOGUE: MAJORING IN MEN

Enjoy Canaan Land in the totality of your life. Marriage. Parenting. Profession. Finances. Education. In every area of your life.

Be a man.

Live the life of maximized manhood.

Christlikeness.

ABOUT THE AUTHOR

Known as "the father of the Christian men's movement," Dr. Edwin Louis Cole (1922–2002) was the founder of the Christian Men's Network. Born in Dallas, Texas, he lived in California for most of his life but returned to Texas to better meet the needs of his expanding ministry.

A former pastor, evangelist, missionary, business executive, and denominational leader, Dr. Cole served the Lord through ministry for more than fifty years, most of those years with his late wife, Nancy, at his side.

The original message God gave Dr. Cole, with which the ministry began, is stated in the book, *Maximized Manhood*. The basic truth of being identified with Christ, which is the essence of salvation, is finding greater application in men's lives today than ever before.

In 1979, CMN started majoring in men in ministry. Since that launch, CMN has reached 210 nations, established 70 national offices, and ministered to millions of men the message of Christlike manhood via Christian Men's events, retreats, church services, videos, radio, television, books, tapes, and satellite broadcasts. Thousands of men have had life-changing experiences, marriages have been resurrected, relationships healed, ministers challenged and encouraged, and over a hundred men's ministries have been birthed. To see men change through the power of the Gospel is the goal. For that purpose, to that end, and for God's glory, Dr. Cole dedicated his life to fulfill God's calling and to impact men with the manhood of Christlikeness.

Over four million copies of Dr. Cole's books are in circulation in more than forty languages. *Maximized Manhood* has sold over one million copies alone.

Christian Men's Network is impacting men everywhere with the message that "Manhood and Christlikeness are synonymous." Under the banner of BUILD MEN RAISE SONS[SM], CMN is committed to create an army of godly men around the world with a goal to recruit and train ten million men in the next decade.

"The malice of today's cultural wars is increasingly hostile. Christianity is now the counter-culture in a post-modern world," states Paul Louis Cole, CMN President. "Ever since Adam blamed Eve and God for his indiscretions, men have found it easiest to go to places of denial and blame. Now it is time to accept the responsibility to change the culture in which we live and change the world."

For thirty years, CMN has fought the battle for the souls of men. Co-founded by the father of the men's movement, Edwin Louis Cole, his wife, Nancy, and his son, Paul Louis Cole, Christian Men's Network calls men into a passionate relationship with Jesus Christ. Ed Cole taught men around the world that "Maturity does not come with age. Maturity comes with the acceptance of responsibility."

Today, Paul Cole continues to add to the vision from a deep conviction that the answer to AIDS, poverty and world hunger is men filled with the Holy Spirit, full of genuine and sacrificial love for God and for people.

The CMN MAJORING IN MEN® Curriculum is currently in use in over 75 nations worldwide. It has been tested by top leaders, by churches from every denominational background and in every conceivable cultural setting.

To host a men's event in your area or at your church, to launch the MAJORING IN MEN® curriculum for your group or to receive information on men's ministry speakers, contact:

Christian Men's Network
P.O. Box 93478
Southlake, TX 76092
cmnoffice@cmnworld.com
1-888-703-1204
www.cmnworld.com

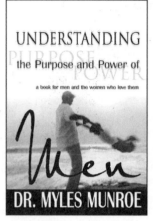

Today, the world is sending out conflicting signals about what it means to be a man. Many men are questioning who they are and what roles they fulfill in life—as a male, a husband, and a father. Best-selling author Myles Munroe examines cultural attitudes toward men and discusses the purpose God has given them. Discover the destiny and potential of the man as he was meant to be.

Understanding the Purpose and Power of Men
Dr. Myles Munroe
ISBN: 978-0-88368-725-3 • Trade • 224 pages

Understanding the Purpose and Power of Men Study Guide
Dr. Myles Munroe

Beneficial for both men and women, individuals and groups, this study guide companion to Dr. Munroe's groundbreaking book will help you to dig deeper into God's proven principles about the critical issue of men's identity.

ISBN: 978-0-88368-855-7 • Trade • 144 pages

WHITAKER HOUSE
www.whitakerhouse.com